ALLIED
ARMORED
FIGHTING VEHICLES
1:72 SCALE

GEORGE R. BRADFORD

STACKPOLE
BOOKS

Published by
STACKPOLE BOOKS
5067 Ritter Road
Mechanicsburg, PA 17055
www.stackpolebooks.com

Cover design by Wendy A. Reynolds

Printed in the United States of America

10 9 8 7 6 5 4 3 2 1

FIRST EDITION

Library of Congress Cataloging-in-Publication Data

Bradford, George.
  Allied armored fighting vehicles : 1:72 scale / George Bradford. — 1st ed.
      p. cm. — (World War II AFV plans)
  Includes bibliographical references.
  ISBN 978-0-8117-3570-4
  1. Armored vehicles, Military—History—20th century—Pictorial works.
2. Tanks (Military science)—History—20th century—Pictorial works. 3.
World War, 1939–1945—Equipment and supplies—Pictorial works. 4. Allied
Powers (1919–)—Miscellanea. 5. Measured drawing. I. Title.
  UG446.5.B6817 2009
    623.7'475—dc22
                                        2009011864

CONTENTS

INTRODUCTION

The eighth volume in this series of books on scale drawings of armored fighting vehicles of World War II is dedicated to 1:72 scale drawings of Allied vehicles and is meant for those AFV modelers who prefer this very popular small-scale product range. These modelers are proud to label it as "Braille Scale," mainly because the parts are so small in some cases that you are almost forced to go by feel.

The drawings are organized in a more or less chronological order, with the earliest at the beginning and the late items at the end of their section. This is by no means a complete coverage of every vehicle from the World War II period, but it will be a great resource for anyone modeling in 1:72 scale and others who merely want a single reference book packed with mutiple-view AFV plans.

The ultimate purpose of this series of books was to try to present a sequence of World War II military vehicle plan-view scale drawings all in one place. Most of these drawings display 4-view plans, but with some of the smaller vehicles, we were able to show five or more views. However, no matter how well the plans are drawn, it will always be necessary to have sufficient photo reference books as well. There are a number of "walk around" and close-up view series on the market to give the super detailers all the finer detail they could ask for.

Over the years, scale drawings of various armored vehicles have appeared in magazines and books, but never all in one place where they would be easy for the researcher or modeler to access them. Many different scales have fought for the limelight, but the more popular ones of late have boiled down to 1:35, 1:48, and 1:72 in the armor-modeling world. With this in mind, we felt that since 1:72 was the second most popular AFV scale, we should publish the series in this smaller scale also.

You will also find a chart at the beginning of this book for reducing or enlarging any of these drawings to other popular scales. The quality and accuracy of modern photocopying should make it possible for you to achieve whatever final scale you require at the lower end of 1:48 and under. However, in some cases where higher enlargement is required, you may find a certain degree of roughness.

These drawings have been created using vector-based drawing applications with line weights ranging from .25 point to 1 point, and thus should easily hold the finer detail when copying. The bulk of these drawings were done over a period of ten years and are currently among the most precise and accurate AFV drawings available. You will also notice a variance in the drawings as the art style changes slightly over the years but eventually supports shading in the majority of the later works.

SCALE CONVERSIONS

REDUCING

1:72 to 1:76 Scale = 95%

1:48 to 1:72 Scale = 66%

1:48 to 1:76 Scale = 63%

1:48 to 1:87 Scale = 55%

1:48 to 1:87 Scale = 55%

1:35 to 1:48 Scale = 73%

1:35 to 1:76 Scale = 46%

1:35 to 1:72 Scale = 49%

1:35 to 1:87 Scale = 41%

ENLARGING

1:72 to 1:35 Scale = 207%

1:72 to 1:48 Scale = 150%

1:72 to 1:16 Scale = 450%

1:48 to 1:35 Scale = 138%

1:48 to 1:32 Scale = 150%

1:48 to 1:16 Scale = 300%

1:35 to 1:32 Scale = 109%

1:35 to 1:16 Scale = 218%

UNITED STATES

M2A4 Light Tank (early production)

By May 1940, the M2A4 Light Tank was finally into production. The eventual output was a mere 365 vehicles and ended around March 1941. An additional ten were assembled about a year later, bringing the total to 375.

Most of these were pressed into service as training vehicles by the U.S. Army during the 1940–42 period. However, 36 were also shipped to England as part of Lend-Lease.

The U.S. Marine Corps also employed the M2A4 as part of its light tank force on Guadalcanal.

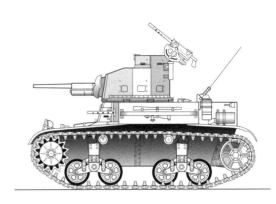

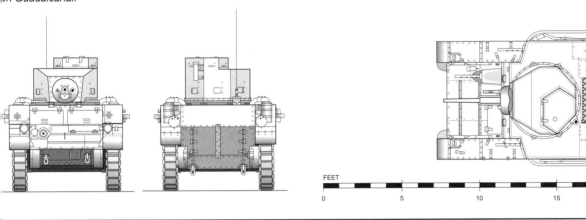

FEET

0   5   10   15   20

1:72 scale

M3A1 White Scout Car (late production)

During World War II, the White Motor Company was producing M3A1 Scout Cars. They were the prewar M3 Scout Car but with a wider hull and the sprung roller on the front. A total of 20,856 were built during the war to serve as anything from armored personnel carriers to command vehicles and ambulances. They came with a removeable tarpaulin top, sometimes referred to as a "tilt."

The M3A1 Scout Cars were supplied to many countries during the war, including Russia and Canada, and also soldiered on in lesser nations well after the war.

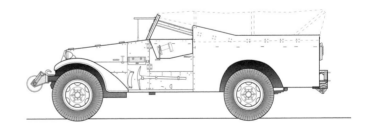

FEET

0   5   10   15   20

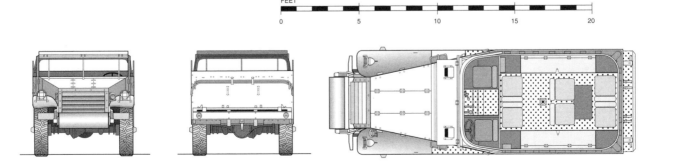

M2A1 Medium Tank

In 1939, the American tank arsenal was among the smallest in the world, rated just below Portugal. The M2 Medium Tank and then M2A1 got the ball rolling, and by 1940, the M3 Medium, with its 75mm main gun, upped the ante again. An order was placed for 1,000 of the M2A1 Mediums, but events in Europe dictated that the M2A1 was far from adequate, and production ended after 126 vehicles, and these were used for training. The M3 Medium with its sponson-mounted 75mm gun would be the workhorse for the early part of World War II.

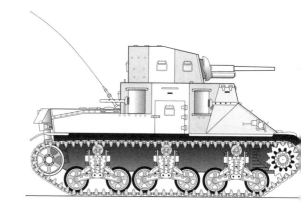

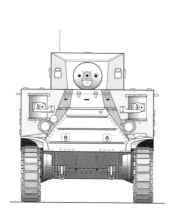
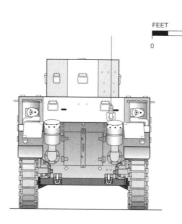

FEET
0   5   10   15

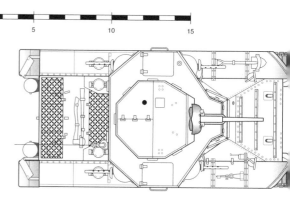

M2 Half-Track Car

This early American half-track, which evolved from the T14, was produced from early 1941 to mid-1943. Powered by a White 160AX engine, it proved relatively simple to produce, and a total of 11,415 came off the line before it was phased out in favor of later models. It was built by both White and Autocar facilities. A characteristic feature of the M2 was the skate rail which ran all the way around its interior rim. The main problem with the M2 seems to be the lack of rear access.

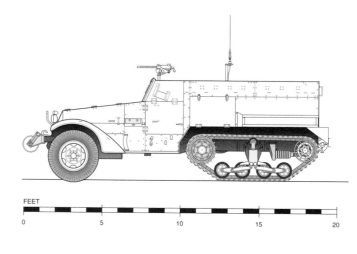

FEET
0   5   10   15   20

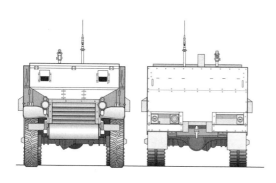
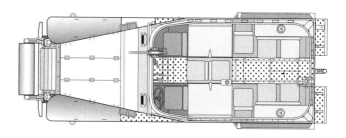

T16 Half-Track Car
Test vehicle built by Autocar

In an attempt to improve the M2 half-track car, the T16, with its extended frame and much larger suspension, was developed. The track width increased from 12" to 14" and the bogies enlarged accordingly. The armored roof was one innovation that was eventually deemed impractical. Any further work on the T16 was stopped in early 1942.

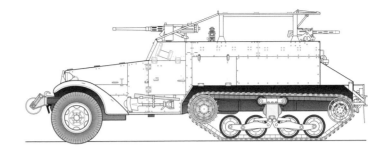

FEET

0   5   10   15   20

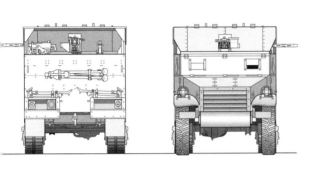

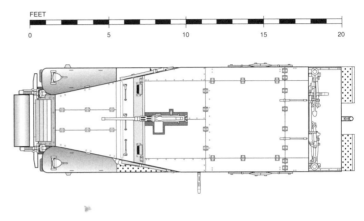

Marmon-Herrington CTMS-1TB1 Light Tank

Among the more obscure American tanks were the Marmon-Herrington Company designs. Most of their orders were for export to Persia, China, and the Netherlands. Included in a 600-tank order from the Netherlands in 1941 was their heavier CTMS-1TB1, which was a 3-man light tank commonly referred to as the "Dutch Three-Man Tank." However, the Japanese swept through the Dutch East Indies before the first deliveries could be made. With America now drawn into World War II, the U.S. Army took control of the M-H series of tanks. They were not impressed, but a few of the CTLS-4TAC light tanks were shipped to Alaska for patrol duty.

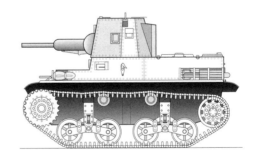

FEET

0   5   10   15   20

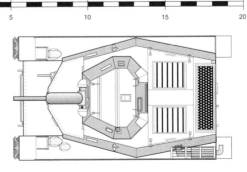

Marmon-Herrington MTLS-1GI4 Light Tank M4-man (Virgie)

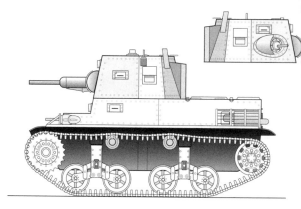

Once again, these tanks were ready for shipment to the Dutch East Indies and were the largest tanks M-H produced. Known also as the "Dutch Four-Man Tank," the hull here was longer and deeper and was fitted with wider track. The 2-man turret mounted twin 37mm guns and a coaxial .30-cal machine gun. There were also ball mounts for machine guns on the front plate.

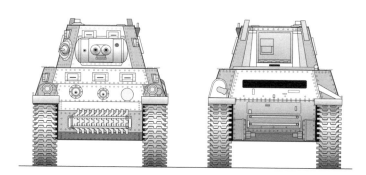

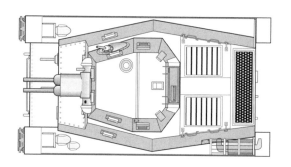

M3 75mm Gun Motor Carriage

Based on the production model gun motor carriage T12, the 75mm M3 GMC went into production by November 1941 in an attempt to quickly field an expedient tank destroyer. The T12 GMC was fitted with a simple gun shield and the old pre-WWI M1897A4 "French 75," mainly because they were readily available. The contract for the M3 was given to Autocar, and by the end of 1941, a total of 86 were delivered to the army. Production in 1942–43 totalled just over 2,000 units. The final batch of 700 used up most of the older M2A2 carriages, since the M2A3 stock had been depleted. Their debut in action in Tunisia was far from impressive, but eventually, when used more as infantry support, they did well.

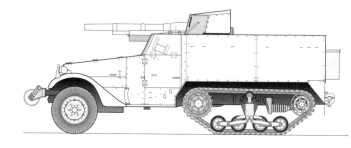

FEET

0   5   10   15   20

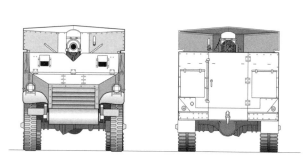

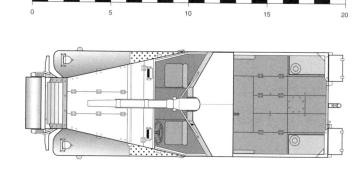

M3 Stuart I Light Tank
Early production

Based on the M2A4, the M3 Light Tank was standardized in 1940. It now sported the trailing idler wheel and lengthened rear superstructure with revised engine compartment. Changes continued to be made throughout production, and the later M3s were quite different. Riveting was replaced by cast and welded turrets and hulls. The sponson machine guns would soon disappear, and a gyrostabilizer would improve gun accuracy. Some were fitted with Guiberson diesel engines, and these would be known as the Stuart II by the British.

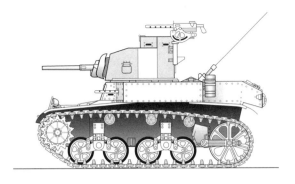

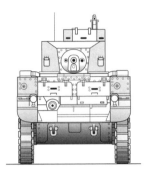

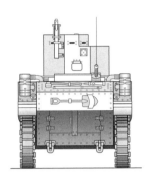

FEET 5 10 15

M3 Lee Medium Tank
An early M3 Medium still fitted with the short 75mm Gun M2

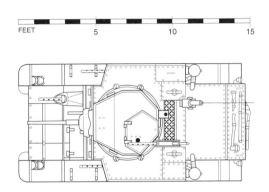

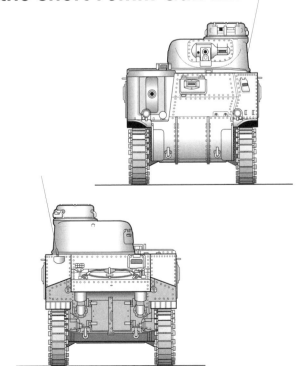

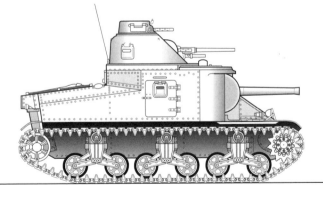

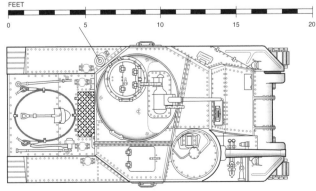

FEET 0 5 10 15 20

M4A1 Sherman Medium Tank
Initial production

The initial-production M4A1s were fitted with the short 75mm M2 gun with double counterweights, which were soon replaced by the longer M3 in the early M34 combination gun mount. The bow sported a pair of fixed machine guns, along with the standard ball-mounted one. The crew had direct vision slots, but periscopes were soon to follow. They also featured the early sighting device on the upper right front corner of the turret, but this too would disappear in favor of a gunner's periscope. It also features the early running gear of the M3 mediums.

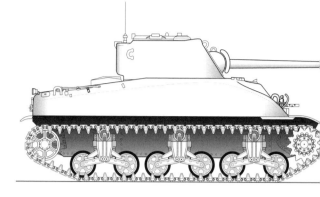

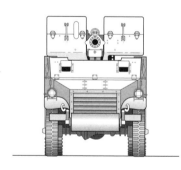

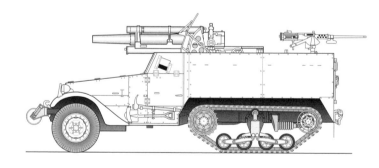

T19 105mm Howitzer Motor Carriage

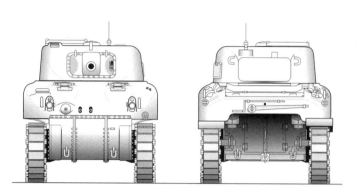

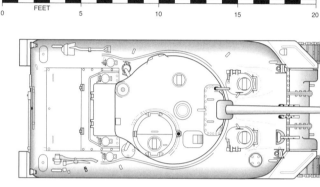

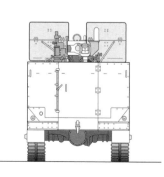

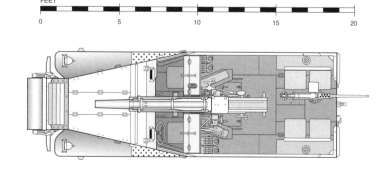

T30 75mm Howitzer Motor Carriage

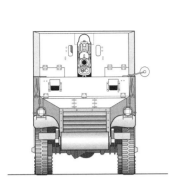
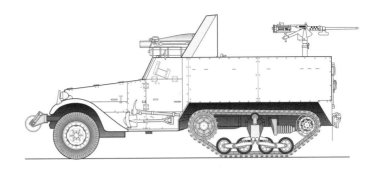
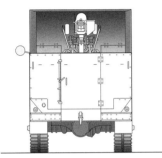

FEET

0   5   10   15   20

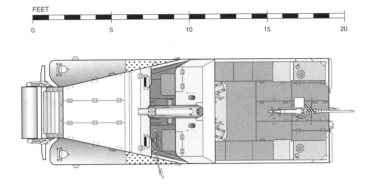

M4 Sherman Medium Tank 75mm (Dry)

With continental R975 radial engine.
Known as Sherman I in British and
Commonwealth service.

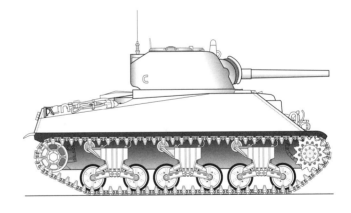
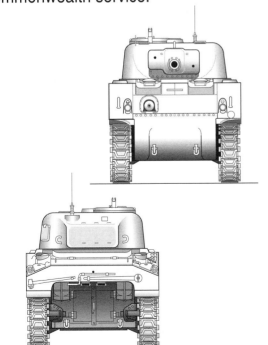
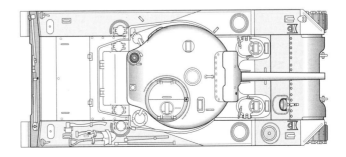

M3 Lee Medium Tank

A late-production M3 Medium with the long
75mm gun M3 and minus the side doors.

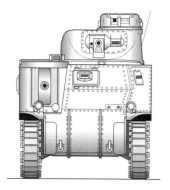

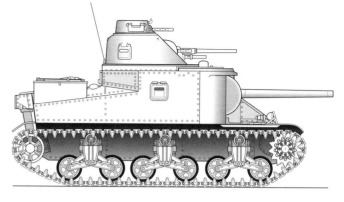

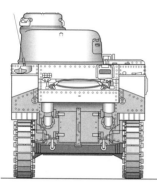

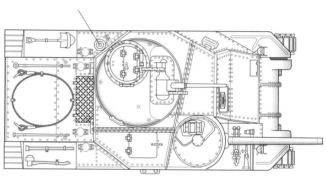

M3A1 Lee Medium Tank

A late cast-hull M3A1 Medium with ventilators
and no side doors.

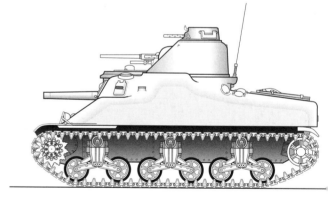

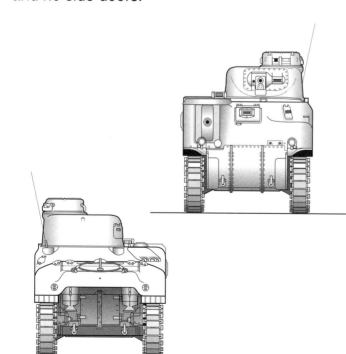

FEET

0   5   10   15

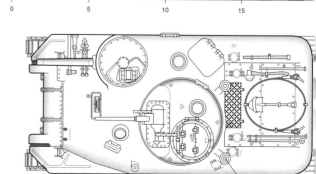

M3A1 Light Tank

Known as Stuart III in British service.

The M3A1 was similar to the late M3 but lacked the turret cupola and had a gyro-stabilized turret basket. Some of the earliest ones still had riveted hulls, but this was merely a cross-over phase, and the majority were welded construction now. About 1,621 were built, with a few hundred having the Guiberson diesel instead of the Continental radial engines. The sponson machine-gun holes were blanked over.

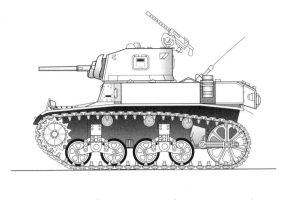

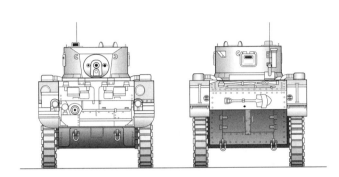

FEET   5   10   15

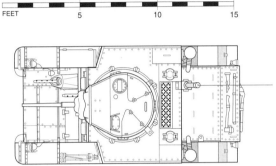

M4A2 Sherman Medium Tank 75mm (Dry)

A mid-production medium tank with GM twin diesel engines.
Known as Sherman III in British and Commonwealth service.

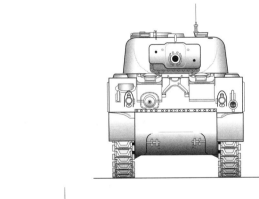

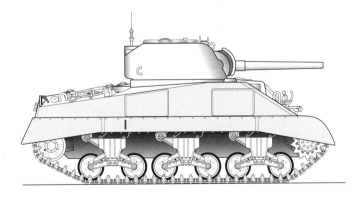

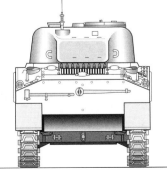

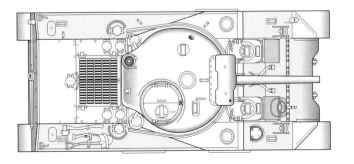

M15 Multiple Gun Motor Carriage

Production began in February 1943, just in time for it to serve with American troops in North Africa, Sicily, Italy, and beyond.

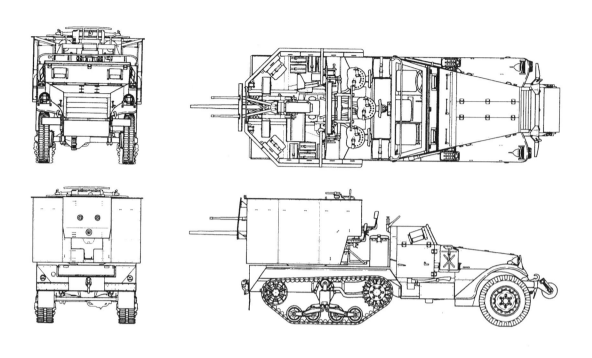

M8 Scott 75mm Howitzer Motor Carriage

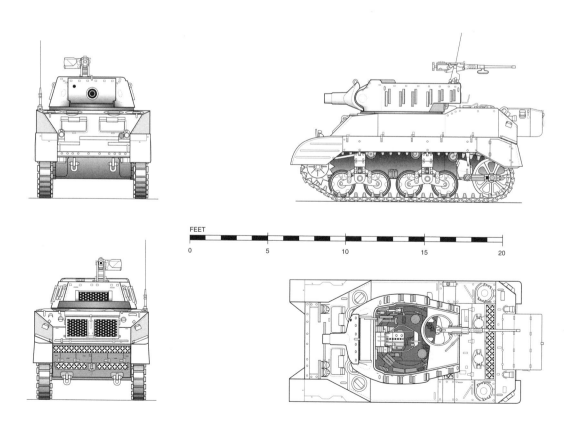

FEET

0　　　　　5　　　　　10　　　　　15　　　　　20

M2A1 Half-Track Car
Built by Autocar & White Motor Company.

Early experiences with the M2 half-track soon demonstrated that the complex skate rail installation for mounting the machine guns simply was not functional. An M32 truck machine-gun mount was chosen in its stead and mounted above the passenger's position over the driving compartment. This became the M49 ring mount in a pulpit arrangement with a .50-cal machine gun, which would soldier on in the later models. Pintle mounts were also fitted at the sides and rear to accommodate the .30-cal machine gun.

Production of the M2A1 version began in late 1943 and on into 1944, and about 1,650 were produced by White Motor Company and the Autocar Company. An additional 5,000 of the original M2 chassis were also refitted as M2A1s.

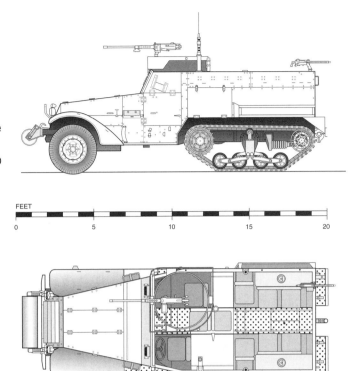

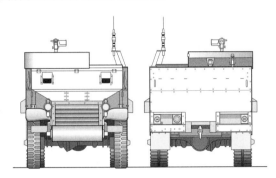

M9A1 Half-Track
Built by International Harvester Company.

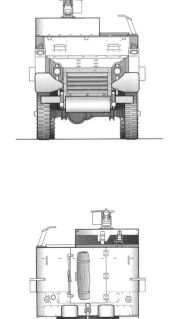

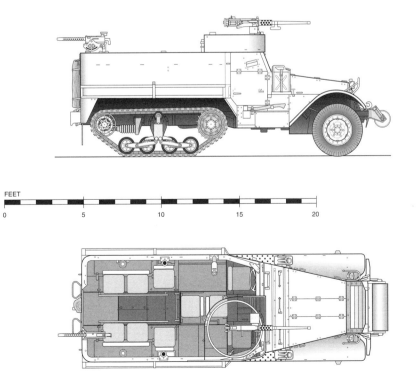

M3A4 Lee Medium Tank

A late-production M3A4 with extended chassis, ventilators, heavy-duty suspension, and Chrysler A57 multibank engine.

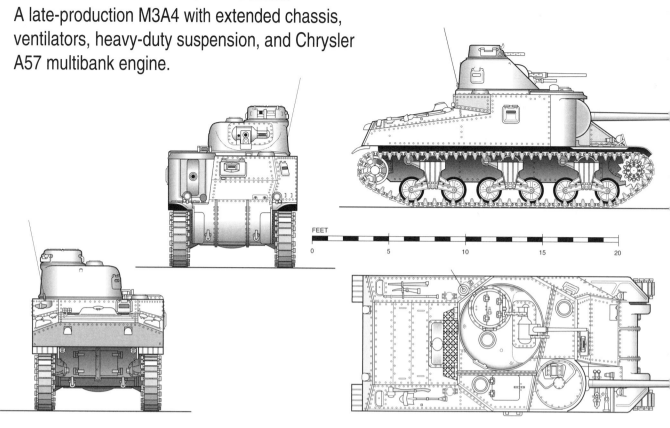

T13 Armored Car

Son of Trackless Tank.

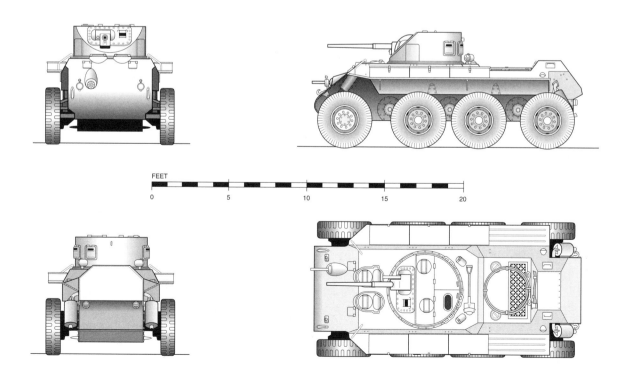

T18E2 Boarhound Heavy Armored Car

Designed for use by the British in the Western Desert, it arrived too late. Thirty were built, but none saw action.

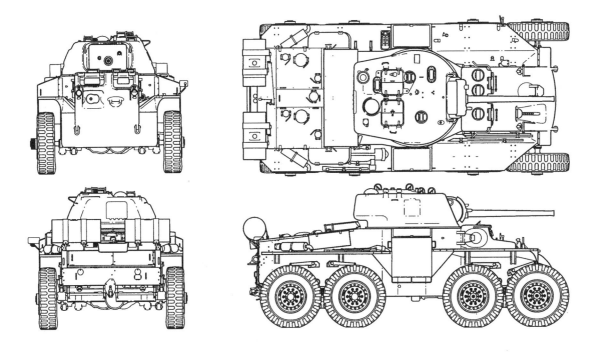

M29 Weasel Cargo Carrier

Early in 1942, G.N. Pyke submitted a plan to the British military which detailed an invasion of Germany through snow-covered Norway. Pyke's plan was to take a small, specialized force and occupy positions in the snowy mountain areas. If they could tie up enough Wehrmacht divisions and keep resources from other German fronts, it may just turn the tables in their favor. Pyke's idea was put through the British Combined Operations Headquarters, and the newly appointed Vice Admiral Lord Louis Mountbatten was very impressed. Pyke's plan was accepted and code-named "Project Plough." Because of Norway's snowy, mountainous conditions, a specially designed snow machine would be needed for commando raids and for the transport of supplies.

On May 17, 1942, the Studebaker Corporation, along with U.S. and British higher ups, set up the specifications for this new snow machine. It was to be able to carry a load of 1200 lbs., travel at a minimum of 30mph (over snow), climb a 30-degree hill, have a range of 225 miles, and last 1,000 miles. It was required to turn in a radius of 12 feet or less and be air transportable and safely dropped by parachute. In case it had to be abandoned, it would also be equipped with a self-destruction device to avoid being captured by the enemy. R.E. Cole, the president of Studebaker, accepted the project, and 34 days later, the first experimental vehicle was ready for testing.

This prototype was shipped from South Bend, Indiana, to Canada's Columbia Glacier in British Columbia. Here the Weasel was put through its paces with Studebaker engineers and men from the 87th Infantry Mountain Regiment. This early pilot was 5 feet wide and a little over 16 feet long. An in-line 6-cylinder engine was mounted amidships with two seats mounted in the center ahead of the engine. The first Weasel weighed in at 7,000 lbs. A power take-off from the engine powered a tunnel-mounted propeller for amphibious use.

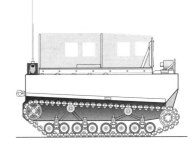

FEET

0   5   10   15

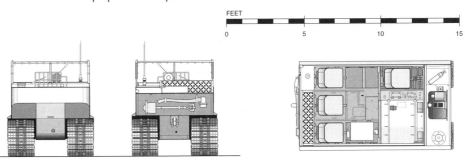

T17 Deerhound
Medium Armored Car

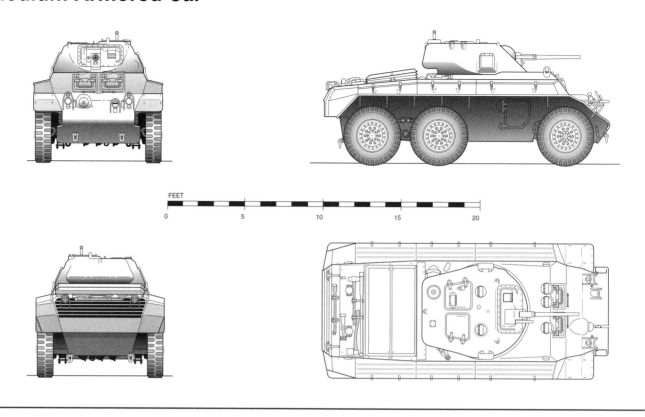

FEET

0   5   10   15   20

T24 Scout Car

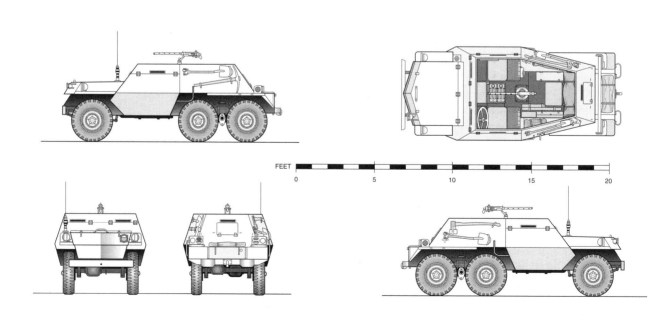

FEET

0   5   10   15   20

T17E1 Staghound Armored Car
In British and Canadian Service

In 1941, the British came to realize a need for a heavier armored car in North Africa. The American T17E1 was eventually chosen and named "Staghound." It turned out to be well liked by its crewmen, and although somewhat heavy for its 37mm firepower, it proved very reliable and easy to drive. Production finally ceased in December 1943, but by that time, 2,844 vehicles had been produced.

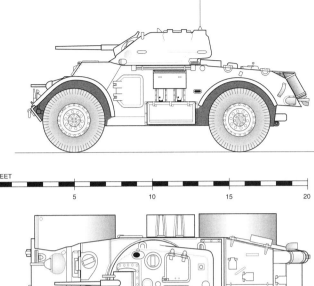

FEET
0   5   10   15   20

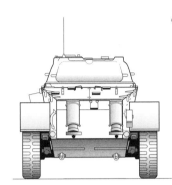

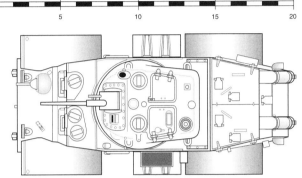

T17E2 Staghound Anti-Aircraft Armored Car
In British and Canadian Service
(Fraser-Nash turret, armed with twin Browning .50-cal machine guns.)

In February 1943, the British foresaw the need for an anti-aircraft version of the Staghound. The standard chassis was fitted with a Norge N80 electrically operated twin-gun Frazer-Nash turret. This new power-operated, open-topped vehicle was too small to accommodate the radio, so the bow machine guns were dropped to make room for it there.

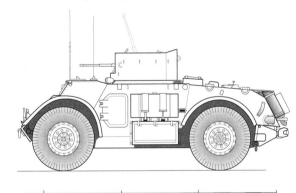

FEET
0   5   10   15   20

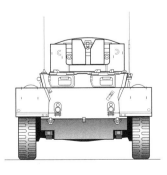

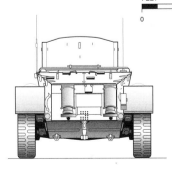

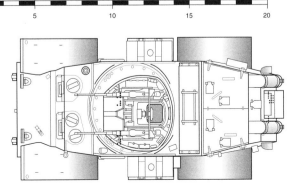

Grant I Cruiser Tank

This was the American M3 Medium Tank built
for British service in North Africa, 1942.

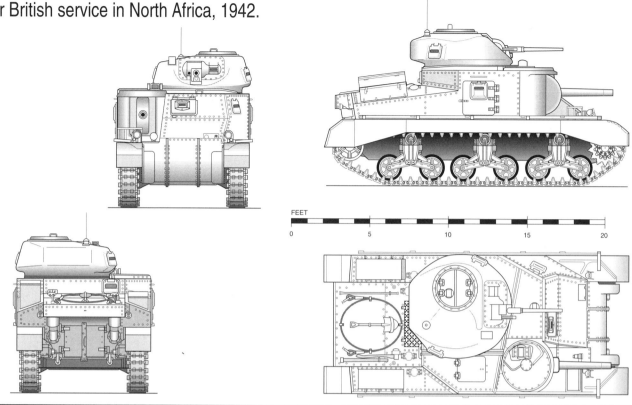

FEET

0   5   10   15   20

M7 Priest Howitzer Motor Carriage

Early production model.

The M7 Howitzer Motor Carriage made its first appearance
in World War II at El Alamein crewed by British troops during
the Operation Supercharge breakout. A few months later,
it was also in action with US troops in Tunisia. The version
shown here was of the early type. Later versions had a
deeper machine-gun pulpit and folding side armor panels
added to better protect the crew and ammunition. The 3-piece
differential and final drive cover were also replaced by the
single-piece sharp-nosed type.

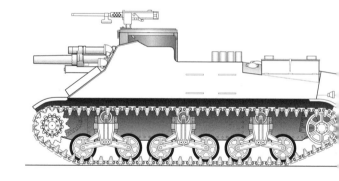

FEET

1   1   2

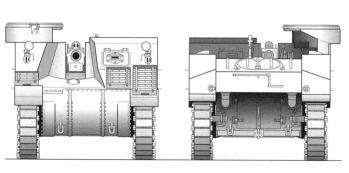

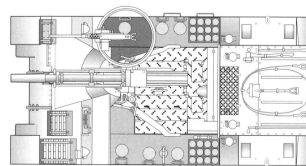

M31 (T2) Armored Recovery Vehicle
On the early M3 medium with dummy guns.

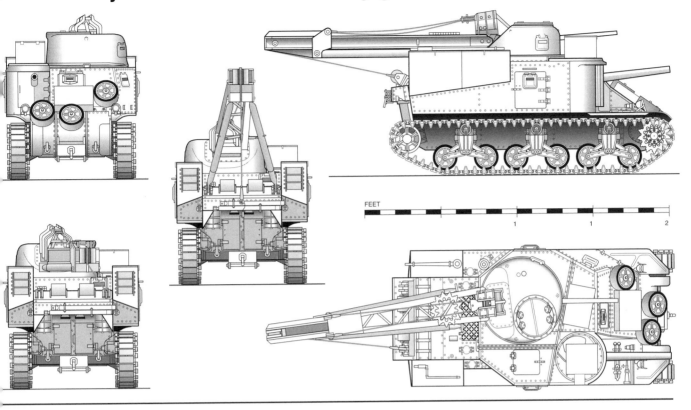

FEET
1   1   2

M8 Greyhound Light Armored Car

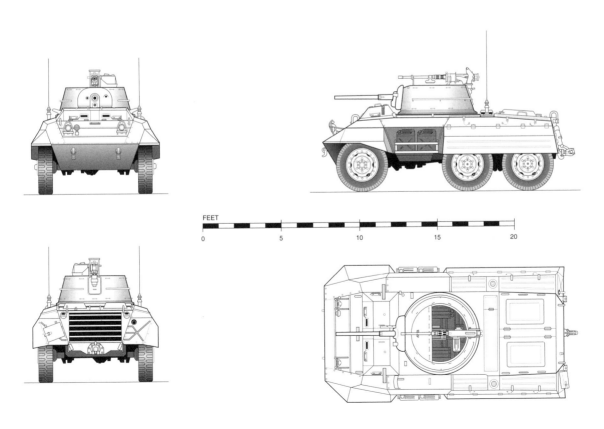

FEET
0   5   10   15   20

M6A1 Heavy Tank
(Welded hull version)

M15A1 Combination Gun Motor Carriage

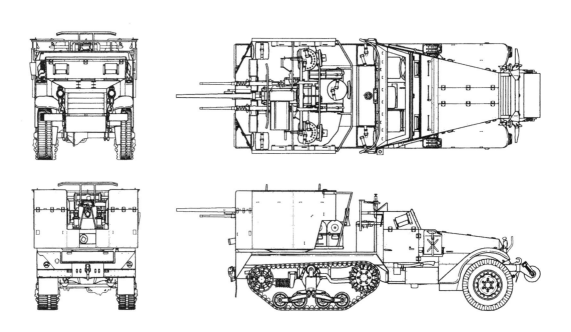

M20 Armored Command Car
(Armored Utility Car M10)

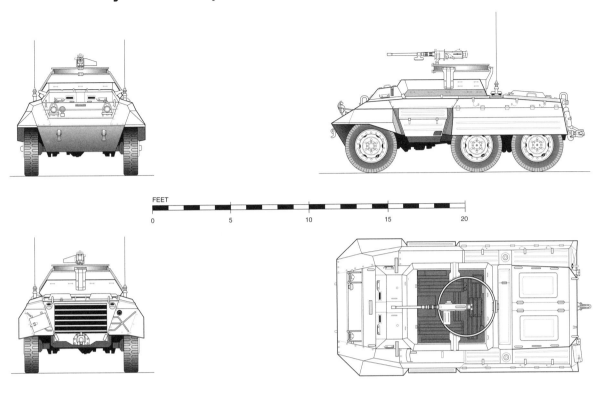

FEET
0   5   10   15   20

M4A3 Sherman Medium Tank 75mm (Wet)
With Ford GAA engine.
Known as Sherman IV in British and Commonwealth service.

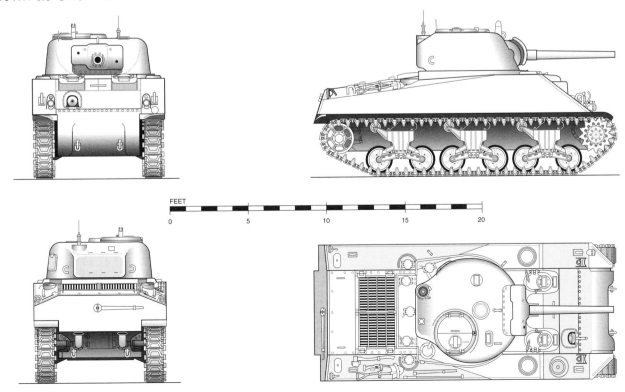

FEET
0   5   10   15   20

M3A3 Stuart V Light Tank

Built to British specifications.

The M3A3 Stuart V was being developed in parallel with the M5 Light Tank. The M3A3 was built more to British specification, and eventually, both Britain and Canada accepted the Stuart V as their standard light tank. They received over 2,100 of these vehicles, and another 1,000 went to Nationalist China, plus 277 to the Free French forces which were by now a sizeable Allied force.

The M3A3 saw service in both Western Europe and Italy and was usually used by armored regiments and reconnaissance regiments to feel out enemy positions on a regimental front.

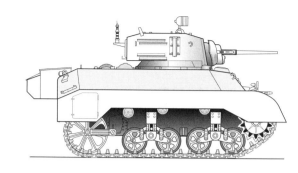

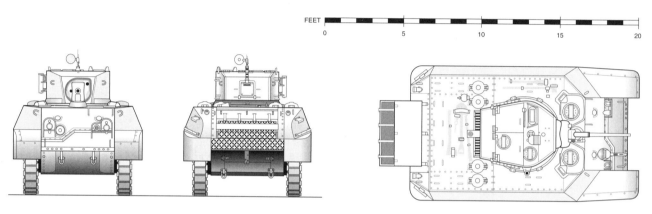

M4A4 Sherman Medium Tank 75mm (Dry)

Remanufactured with Chrysler A57 multibank engine.
Known as Sherman V in British and Commonwealth service.

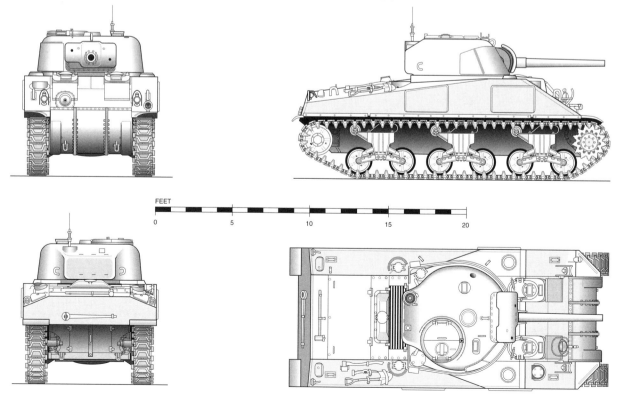

M12 155mm
Gun Motor Carriage

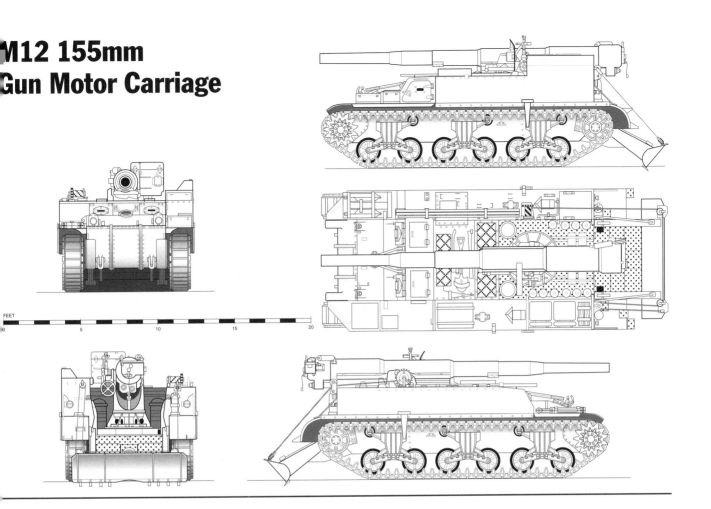

FEET
0   5   10   15   20

M30 Cargo Carrier

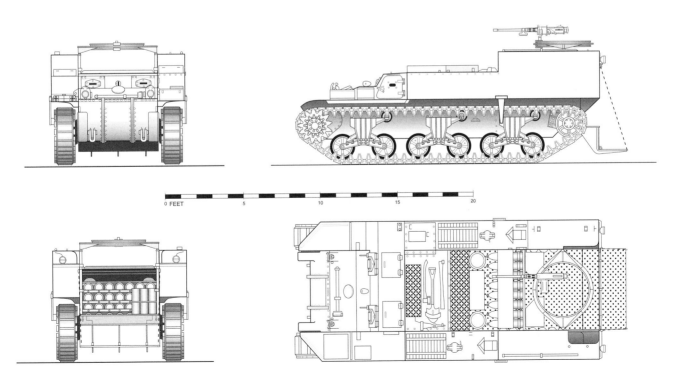

0 FEET   5   10   15   20

M5A1 Stuart VI Light Tank
Early production. Fitted with Culin hedgerow cutter.

The M5 light tank evolved from the M3E3, and to avoid confusion with the M4 medium tanks, it was wisely designated as M5 Light Tank rather than repeating M4. Production began in April 1942, and roughly 2,074 were produced by December of that year. The new improved turret developed from the M3A3 provided room for an SCR 508 radio in the rear bustle, and a similar approach was taken with the M5A1 turret. By June 1944, a total of 6,810 of the M5A1 model had been built.

The M5A1 was chosen for the U.S. Army, and the M3A3 was directed to foreign aid. However, once production allowed, the M5A1 Stuart VI was also issued to British units. This M5A1 is fitted with the Culin hedgerow cutter, a device welded together from German angle iron beach obstacles. Its purpose was to cut through the roots of the Normandy hedgerows. They were named after Sgt. Curtis Culin, who first created this ingenious device.

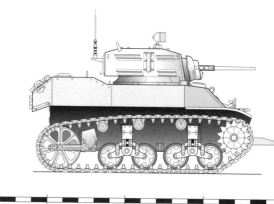

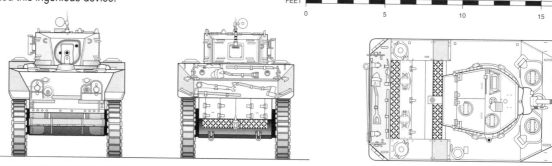

M10 3-inch Gun Motor Carriage
Mid-production

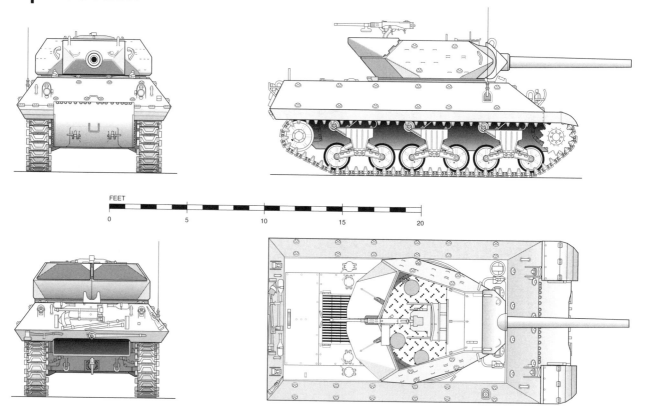

M4A1(76)W Sherman Medium Tank

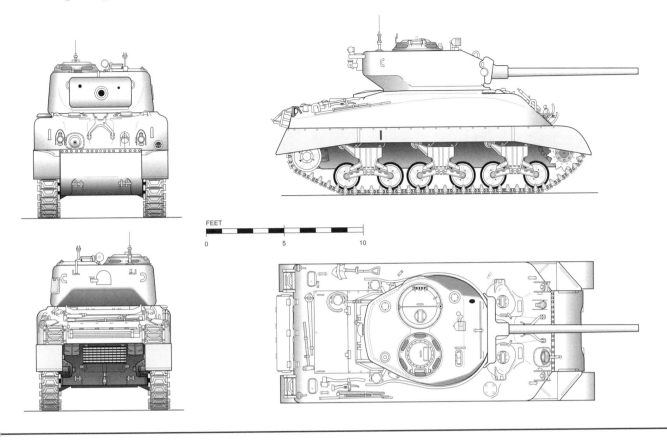

FEET

0　　　　　5　　　　　10

M4A3E2 Jumbo Assault Tank

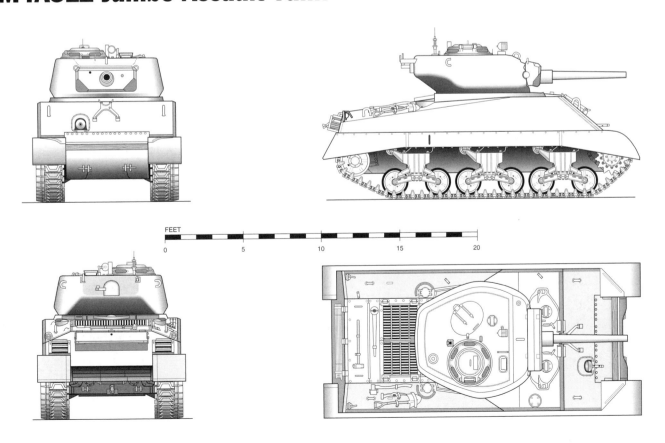

FEET

0　　　5　　　10　　　15　　　20

M18 Hell Cat 76mm Gun Motor Carriage

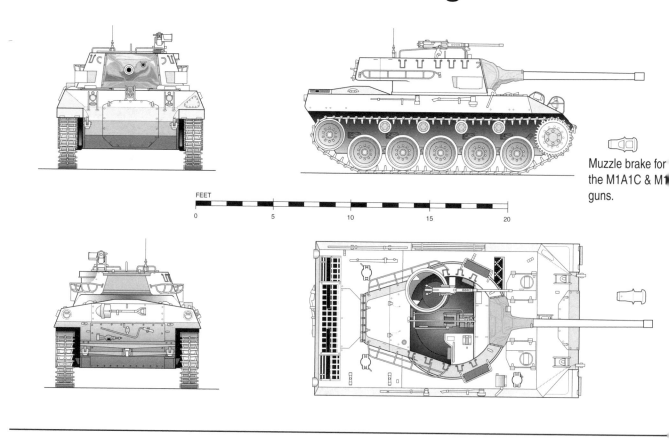

FEET

0   5   10   15   20

Muzzle brake for
the M1A1C & M1
guns.

M3A2 Half-Track

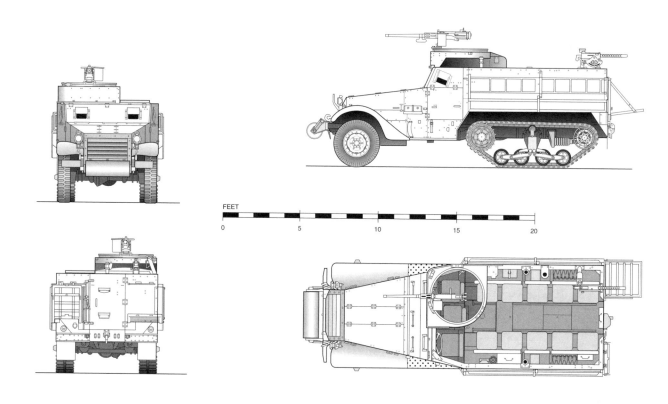

FEET

0   5   10   15   20

M4A2(76)W Sherman Medium Tank

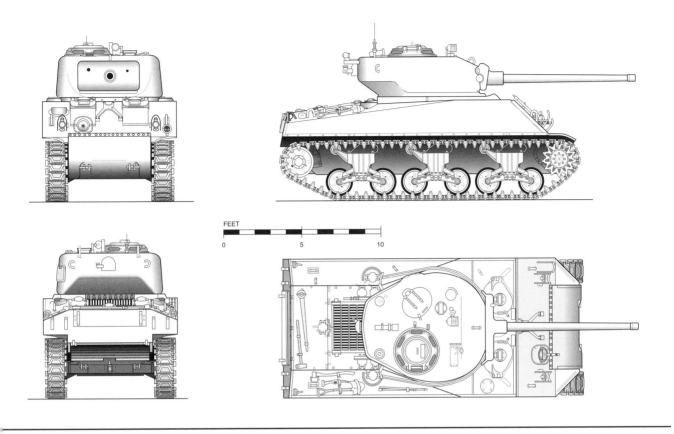

FEET

0   5   10

M39 Armored Utility Vehicle

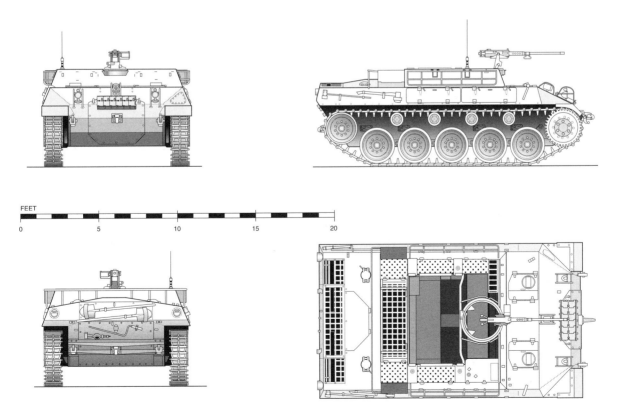

FEET

0   5   10   15   20

M24 Chaffee Light Tank

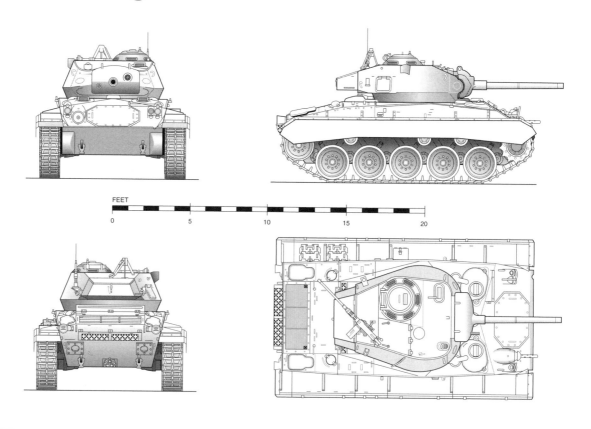

FEET

0   5   10   15   20

M22 (T9E1) Locust Light Tank

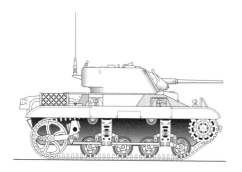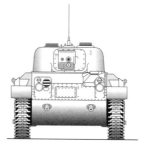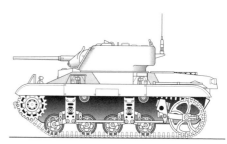

The requirement for an airborne light tank had been seeded in the US well before it entered World War II. Plans were submitted in 1941, and acceptance was given to the Marmon-Herrington design. The weight limit was set at 7.5 tons, but by the time the first T9 prototype appeared, it was obvious that 8 tons was more realistic. By November 1942, the first T9E1 was at APG for testing, and 500 were ordered. Production began in April 1943 for a total production of 830 vehicles, now standardized as M22. In the end, these little tanks never did see action with US forces; however, a few were used by the British 6th Airborne for the Rhine crossing of March 24, 1945.

FEET

0   5   10   15   20

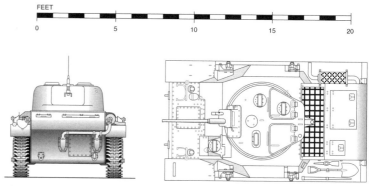

LVT(A)-1 Amphibious Landing Vehicle
Landing Vehicle Tracked (Armored) Mk. 1

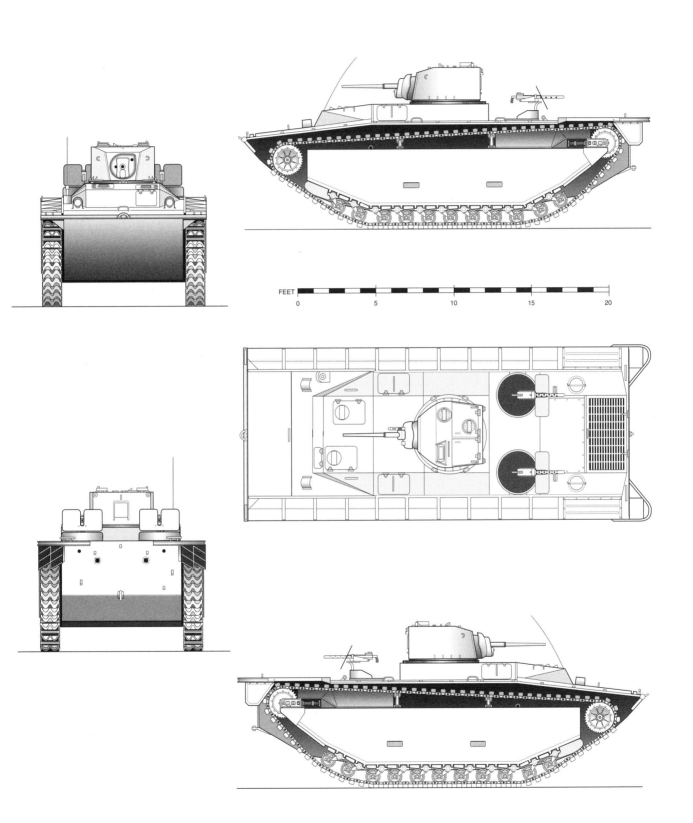

FEET

0   5   10   15   20

LVT(A)-4 Amphibious Landing Vehicle
Landing Vehicle Tracked (Armored) Mk. 4

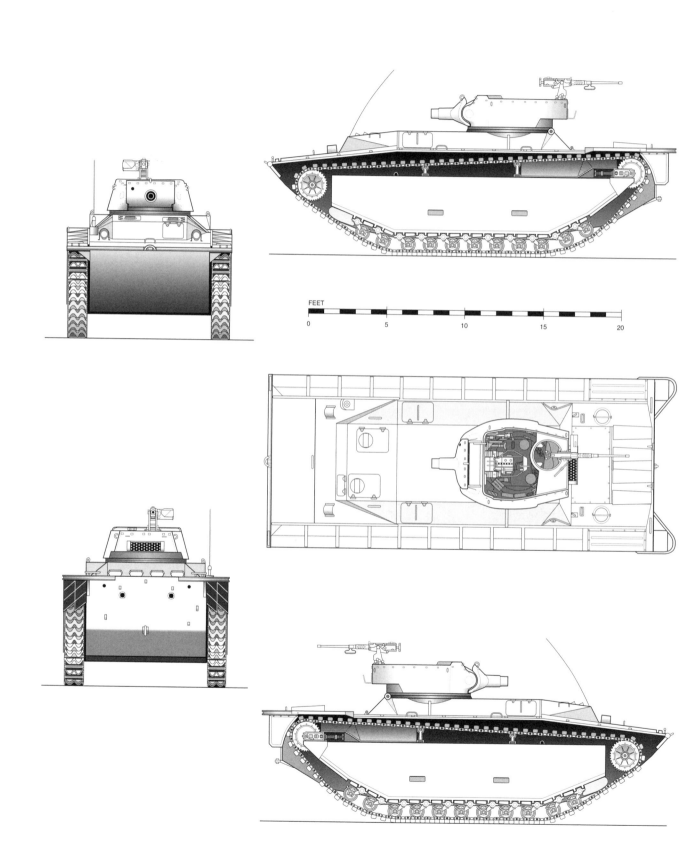

FEET

0   5   10   15   20

T1E3 Aunt Jemima
Sherman Mine Exploder

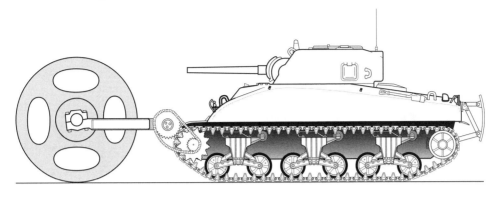

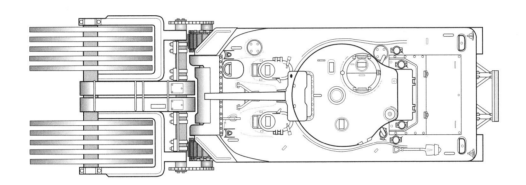

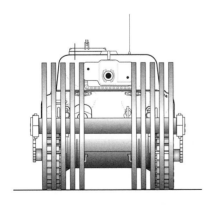

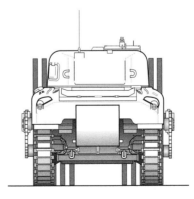

The T1E3 Aunt Jemima mine roller was one of many attempts at mine clearing late in the war. Unfortunately, the weather dictated when and where these heavy brutes could be used, and the fall, winter, and spring of 1944–45 were far from ideal. Once they were mired in, it took an army of recovery crews to get them out. There were at least twenty-seven T1E3s supporting the 702nd and 744th Tank Destroyer Battalions during July 1944 for Operation Cobra, and most continued to serve well beyond that period.

M36 90mm Gun Motor Carriage

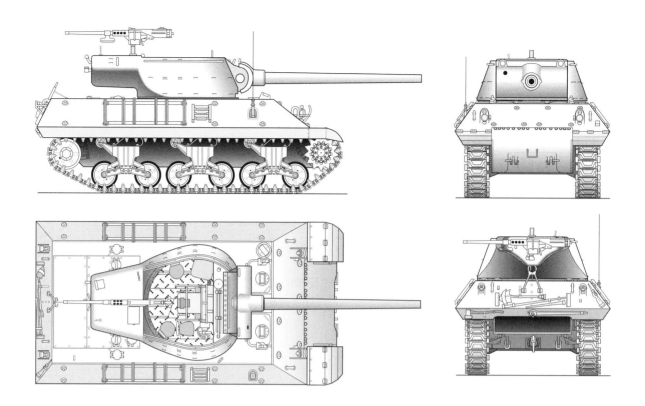

M36B1 90mm Gun Motor Carriage

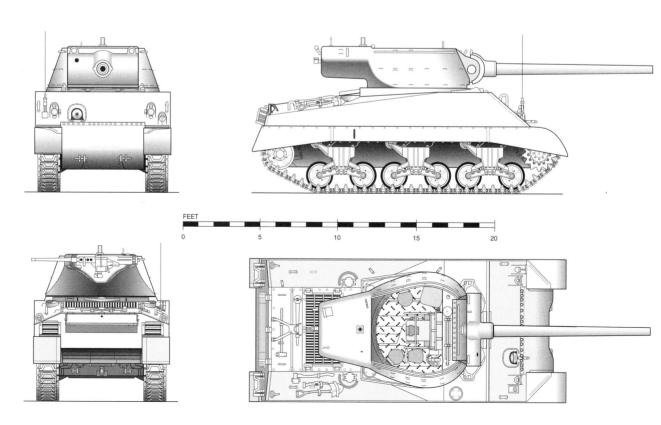

FEET

0　　　　　5　　　　　10　　　　　15　　　　　20

M37 105mm Howitzer Motor

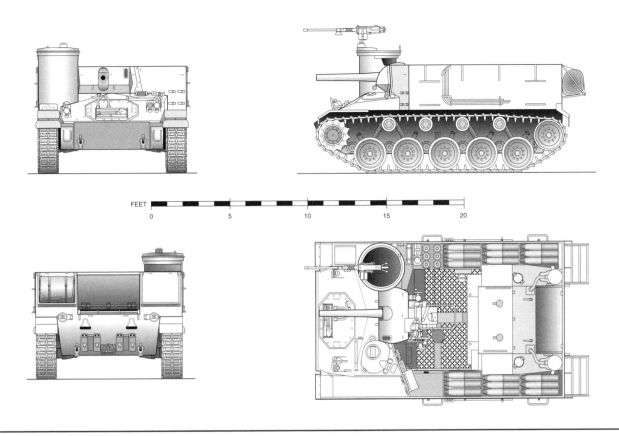

FEET
0 5 10 15 20

Sherman Calliope
T34 Rocket Launcher

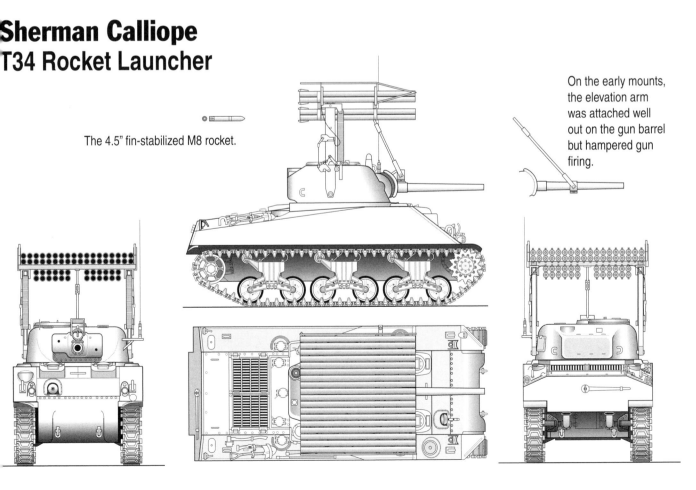

The 4.5" fin-stabilized M8 rocket.

On the early mounts, the elevation arm was attached well out on the gun barrel but hampered gun firing.

GMC DUKW-353
(Inital production model)

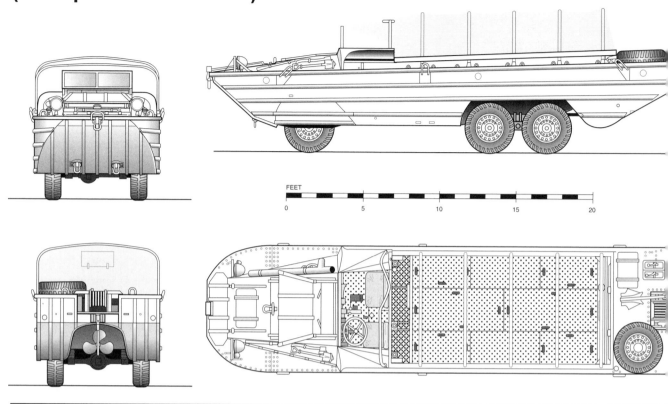

FEET

0   5   10   15   20

M29C Weasel Cargo Carrier

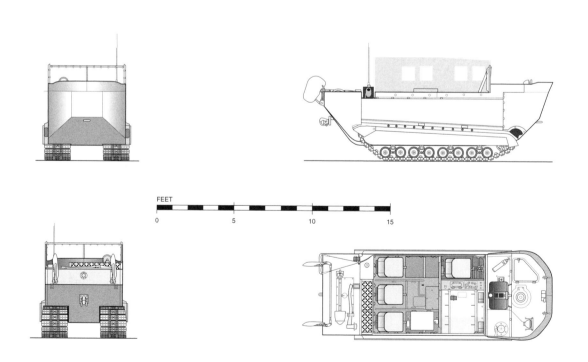

FEET

0   5   10   15

M4A3(76)W HVSS Sherman (Often referred to as M4A3E8)

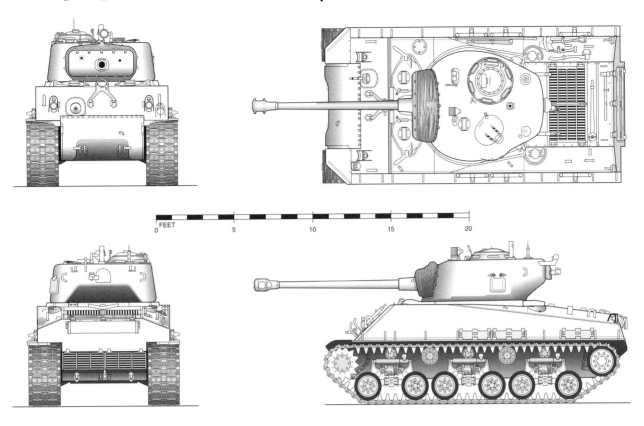

FEET
0   5   10   15   20

M26 Pershing Medium Tank

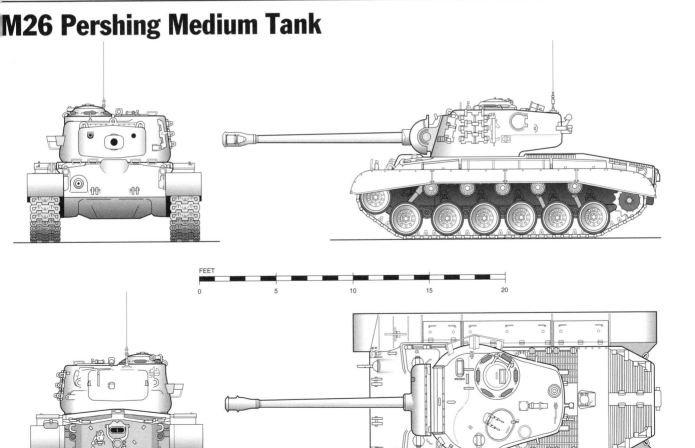

FEET
0   5   10   15   20

T26E4 Super Pershing
Temporary Pilot No. 1, Europe, April 1945, 3rd Armored Division.

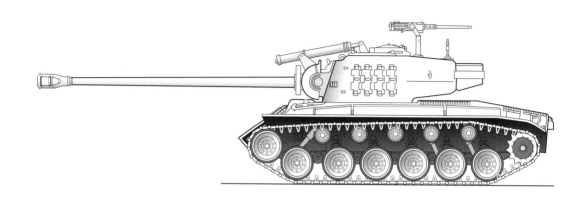

FEET

0   5   10   15   20

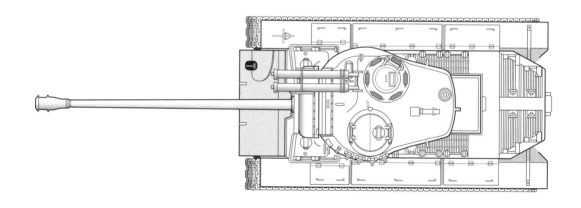

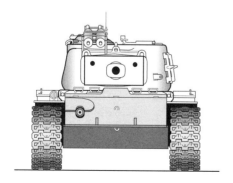

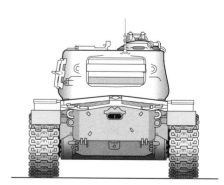

T28 Superheavy Tank
(105mm Gun Motor Carriage T95)

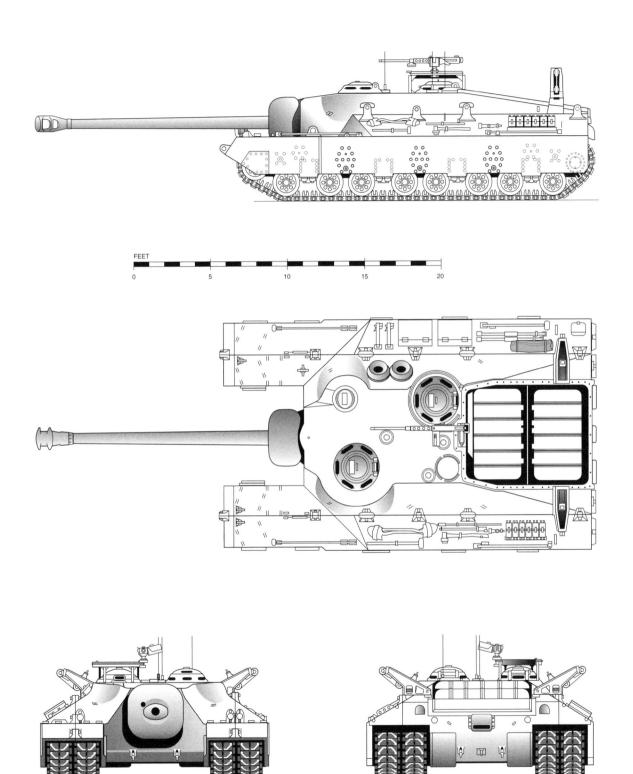

FEET

0   5   10   15   20

Vickers Medium Mk. II** Tank

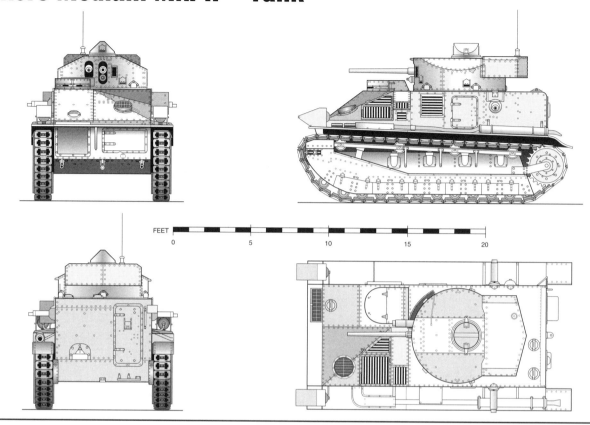

FEET

0   5   10   15   20

Rolls-Royce Armored Car
1924 pattern used in North Africa, 1940.

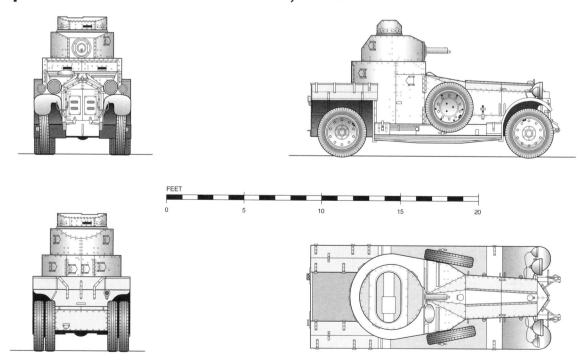

FEET

0   5   10   15   20

Mk. I Cruiser Tank (A9)

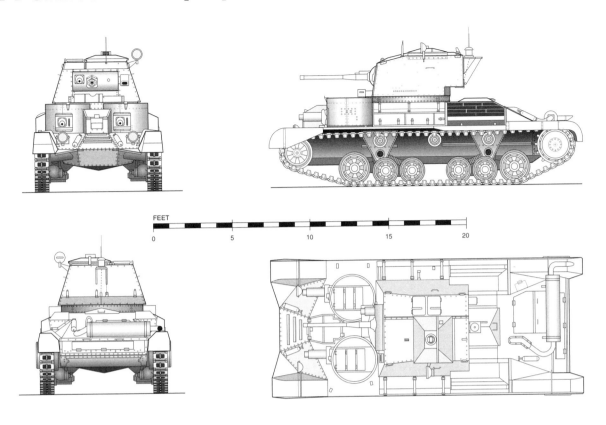

Morris Model CS9/LAC
Armored Reconnaissance Car
11th Hussars, North Africa, 1940.

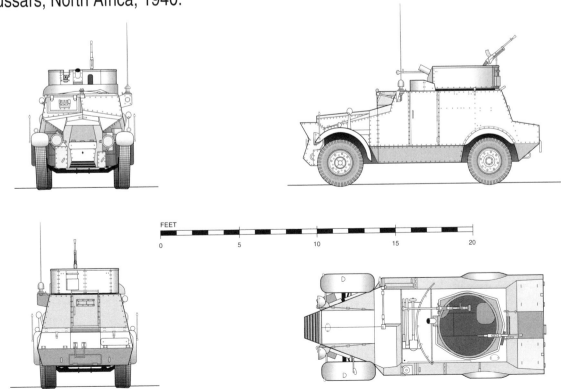

Matilda Infantry Tank Mk. I (A11)

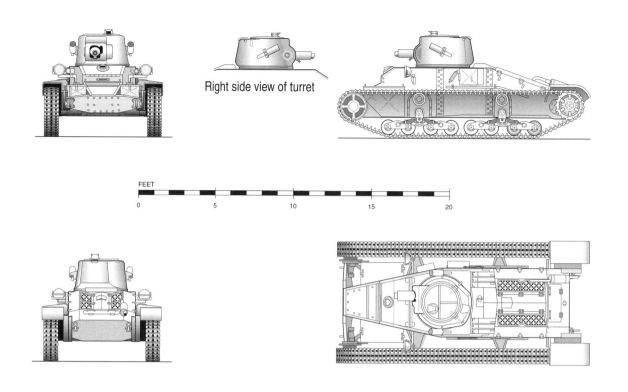

Right side view of turret

FEET
0   5   10   15   20

Mk. III Cruiser Tank (A13 Mk. I)

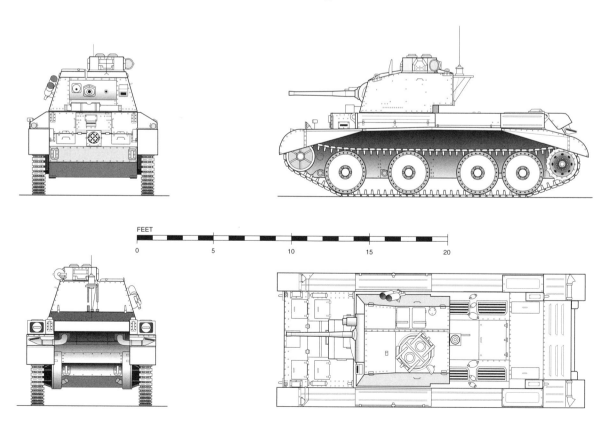

FEET
0   5   10   15   20

Mk. IV Cruiser Tank (A13 Mk. II)

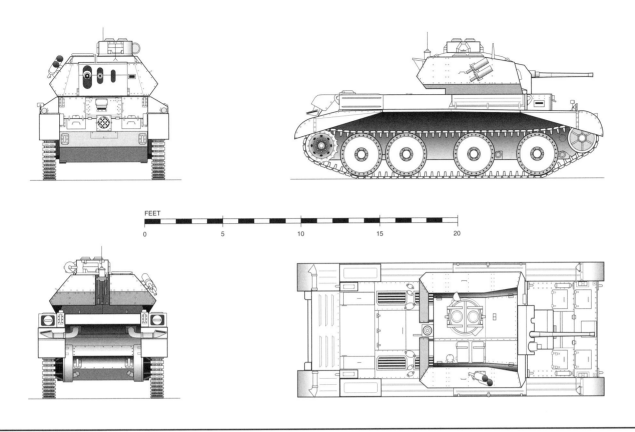

FEET

0   5   10   15   20

Mk. IVA Cruiser Tank (A13 Mk. II)

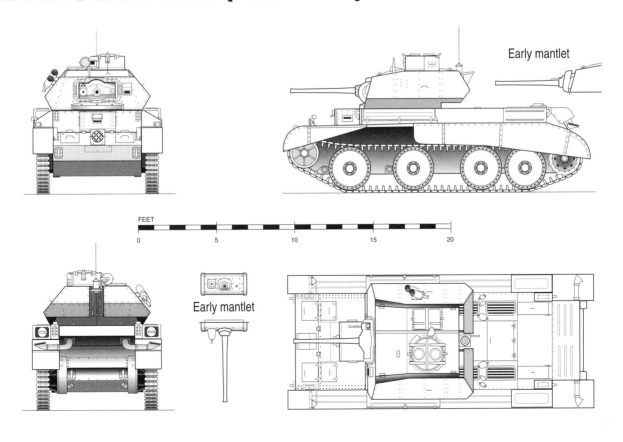

Early mantlet

Early mantlet

FEET

0   5   10   15   20

Universal Carrier No. 1, Mk. I

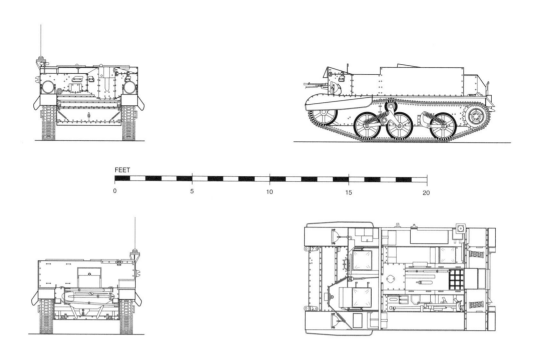

FEET

0   5   10   15   20

Mk. IIA Cruiser Tank (A10)

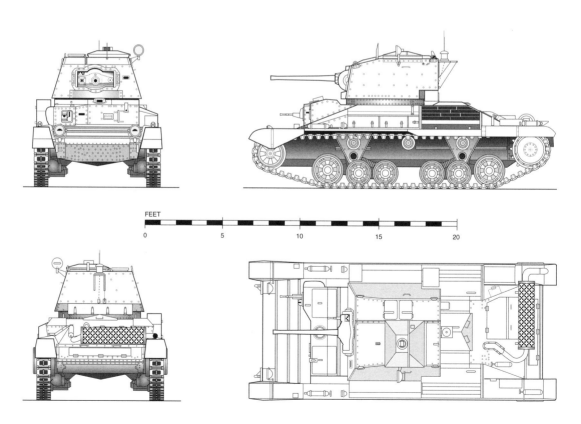

FEET

0   5   10   15   20

Ford Indian Pattern Carrier Mk. IIA

Armored Carrier, Wheeled, I.P. Mark IIA.

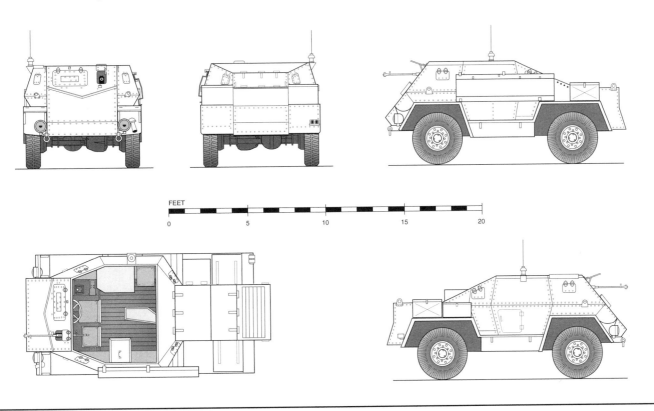

FEET

0   5   10   15   20

Matilda Infantry Tank Mk. IIA (A12)

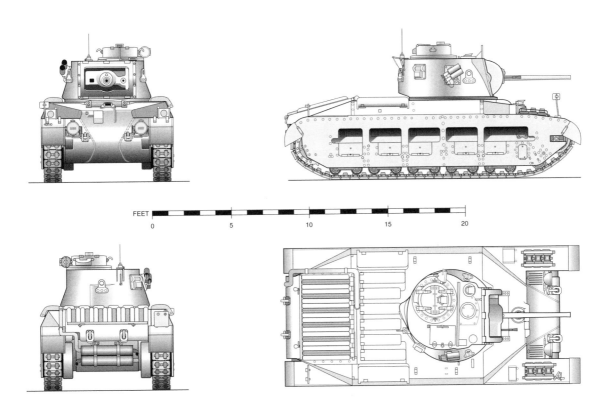

FEET

0   5   10   15   20

Mk. VIA Light Tank

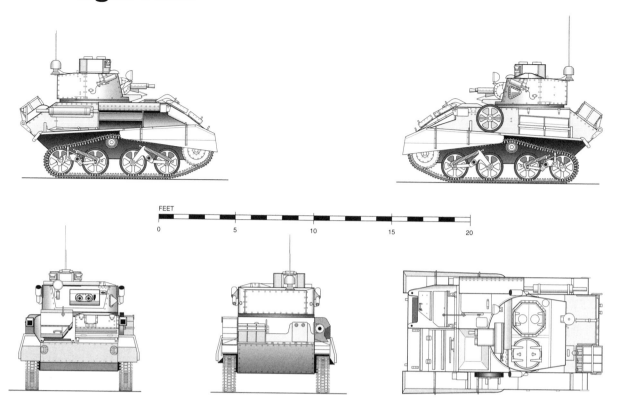

FEET

0   5   10   15   20

Mk. VIB Light Tank

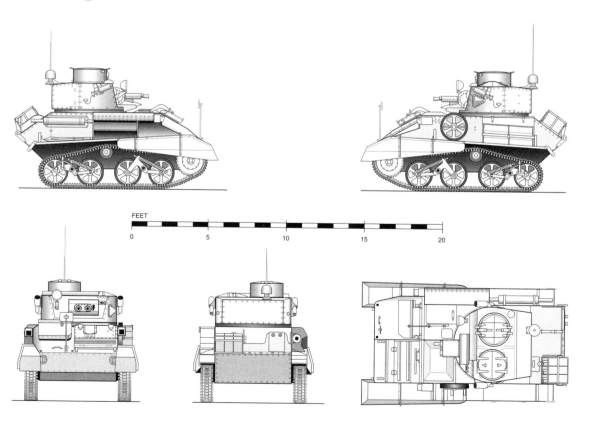

FEET

0   5   10   15   20

Mk. V** Cruiser Tank (A13 Mk. III**)
Covenanter III

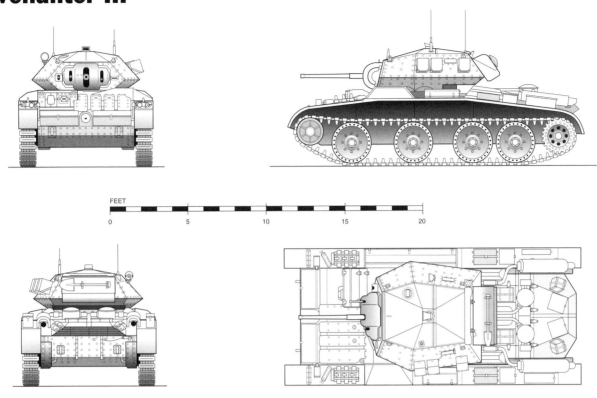

FEET
0   5   10   15   20

Humber Light Recon Car Mk. III

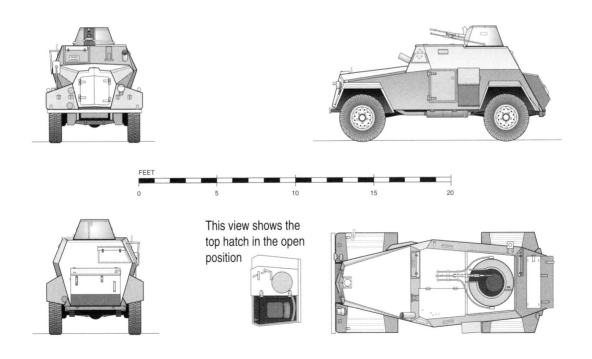

FEET
0   5   10   15   20

This view shows the top hatch in the open position

Mk. VI Cruiser Tank (A15)
Crusader I

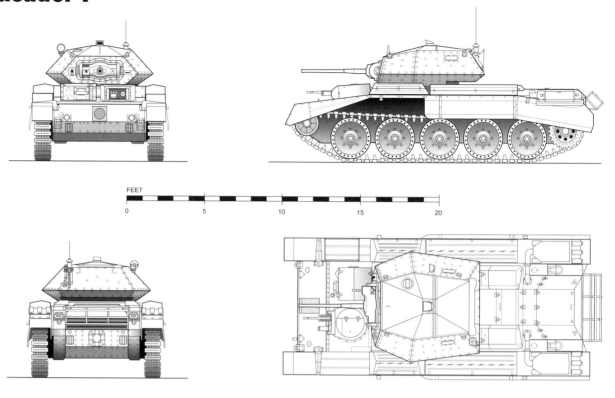

FEET

0   5   10   15   20

Mk. VIA Cruiser Tank (A15)
Crusader II

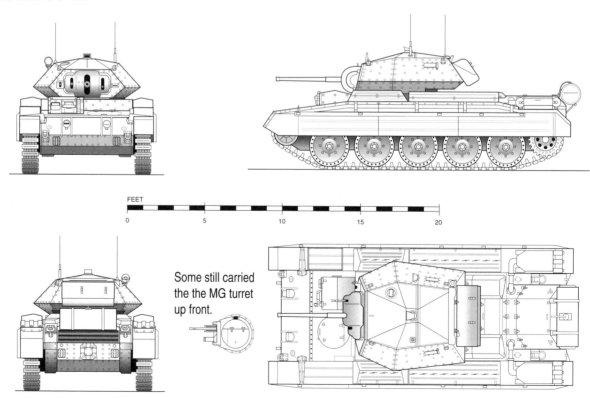

FEET

0   5   10   15   20

Some still carried the the MG turret up front.

ren Carrier No. 2 Mk. I (A15)

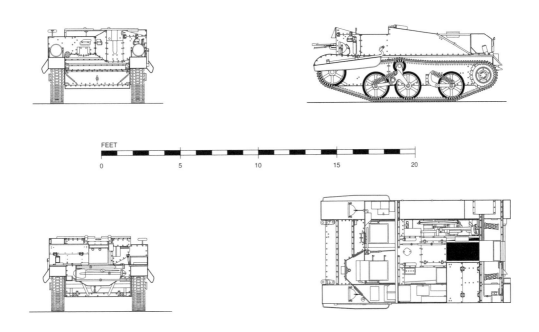

FEET

0   5   10   15   20

Light Reconnaissance Car
Beaverette Mk. III

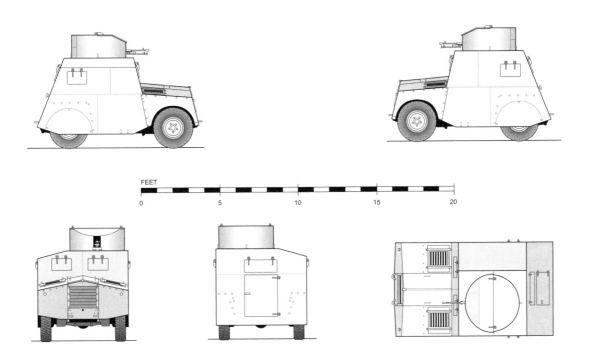

FEET

0   5   10   15   20

Humber Scout Car Mk. I

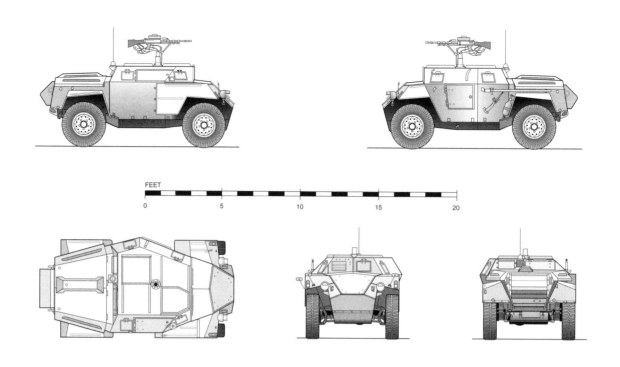

FEET
0   5   10   15   20

Grant I Cruiser Tank

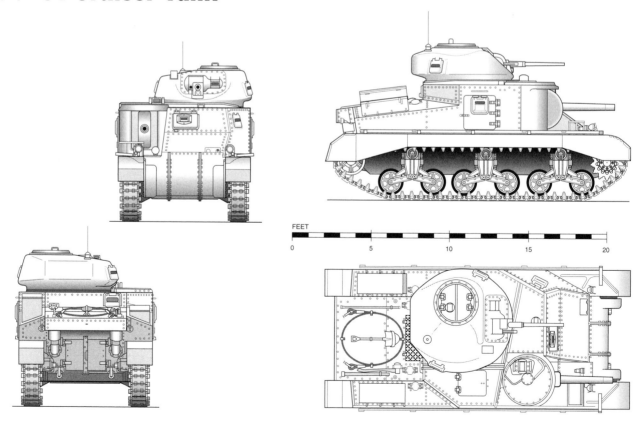

FEET
0   5   10   15   20

Stuart I Light Tank (M3) Honey, early production

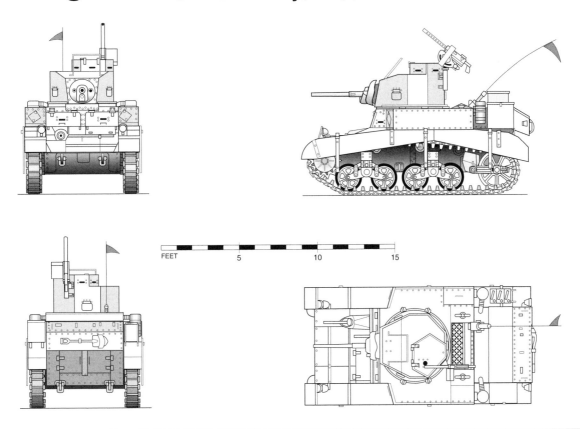

FEET 5 10 15

Mk. II Anti-Aircraft Light Tank

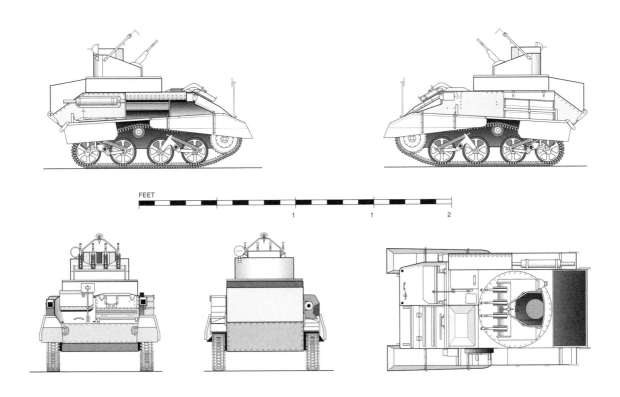

FEET 1 1 2

AEC Dorchester Armored Command Vehicle

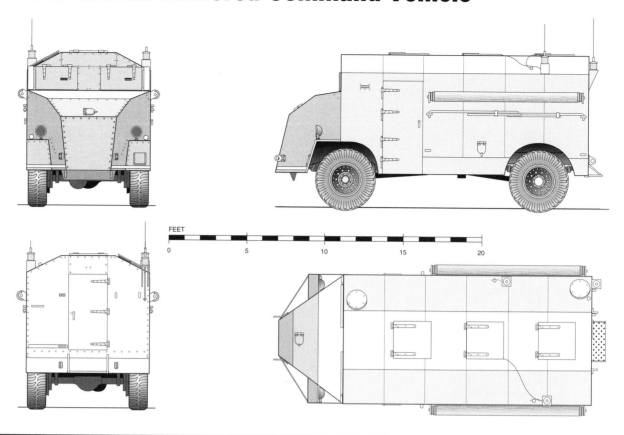

FEET

Mk. III Infantry Tank
Valentine II

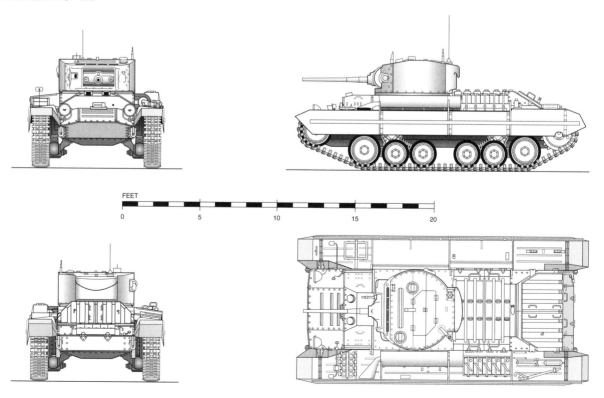

FEET

Mk. IIA* Infantry Tank (A12)
Matilda IV

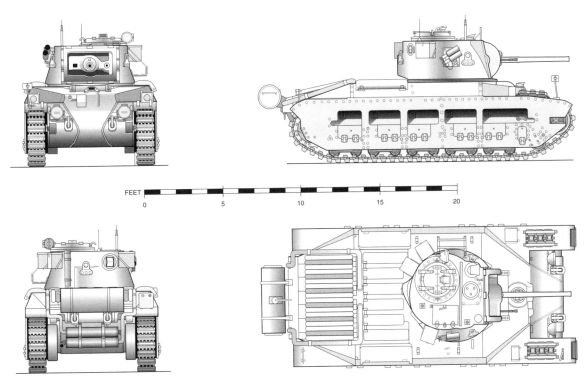

FEET

0   5   10   15   20

Daimler Mk. I Armored Car

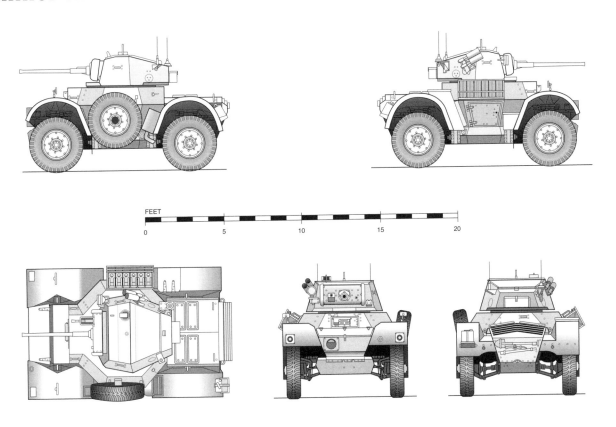

FEET

0   5   10   15   20

Bishop Self-Propelled 25-pdr

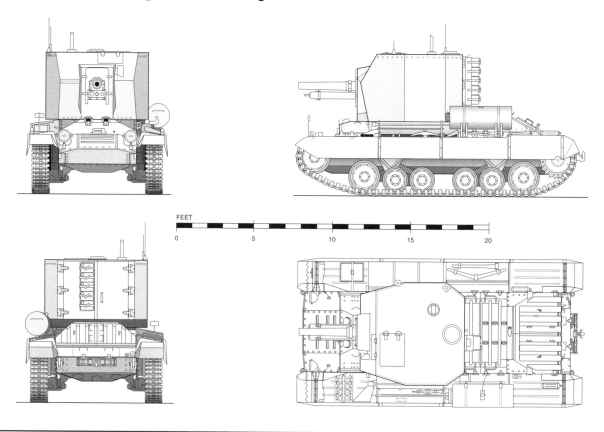

Mk. VI Cruiser Tank (A15)
Crusader III

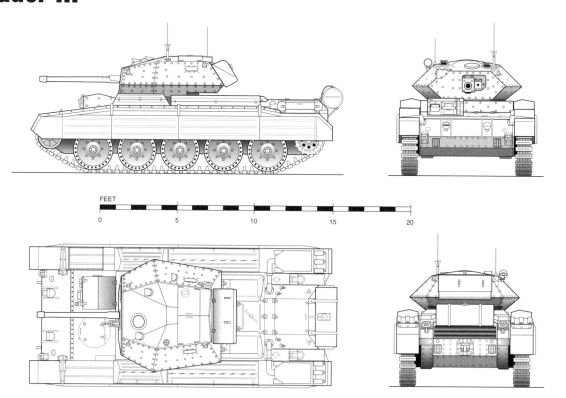

AEC Carrier for 6-pdr Gun Mk. I, Deacon

The flowing battles in North Africa soon made it clear that a self-propelled anti-tank gun was a must. One of the solutions was to mount the trusty 6-pounder anti-tank gun on the back of the AEC Matador armored ammunition carrier. 175 of these conversions were built and saw service with British forces until the end of the Desert War, when they were turned over to Turkey.

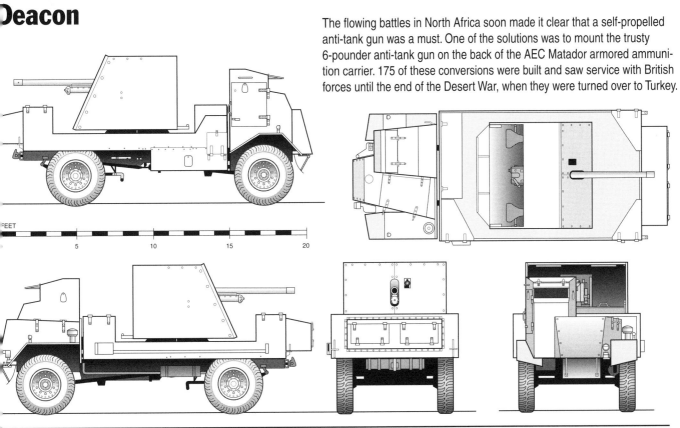

FEET
5   10   15   20

Daimler Scout Car Mk. II

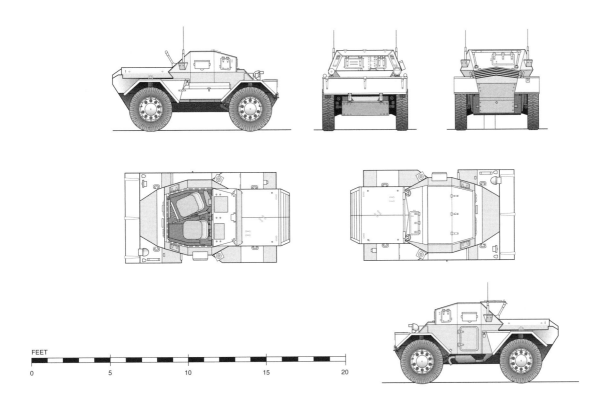

FEET
0   5   10   15   20

Mk. IV Infantry Tank (A22)
Churchill Mk. I with 3" howitzer in hull front

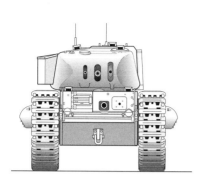
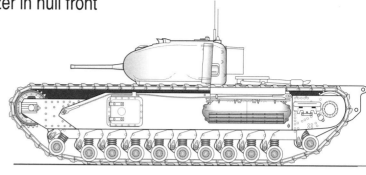
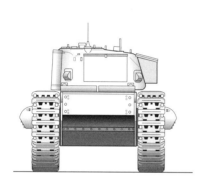
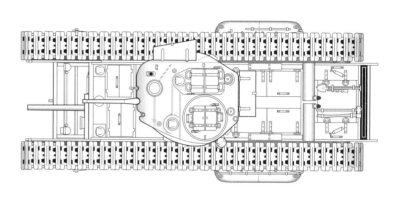

Mk. IV Infantry Tank (A22)
Churchill Mk. II (Upgraded)

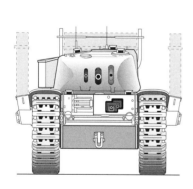
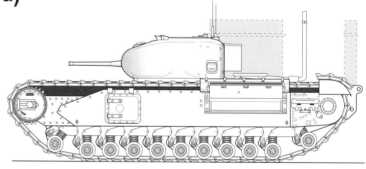
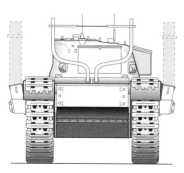
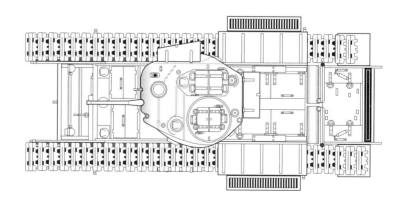

Staghound III Armored Car
(U.S. T17E3)

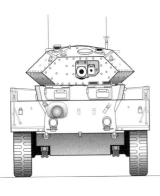

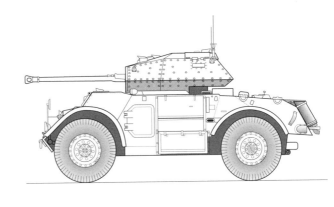

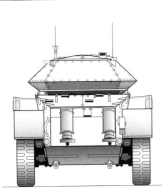

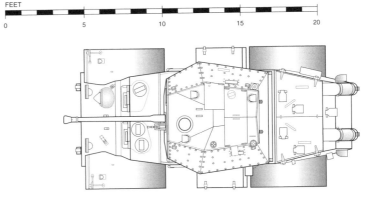

FEET

0   5   10   15   20

Mk. III Infantry Tank
Valentine Mks. III & V

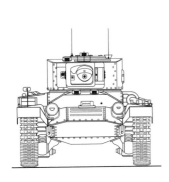

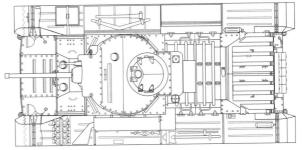

FEET

0   5   10   15   20

Mk. IV Cruiser Tank (A27M)
Cromwell

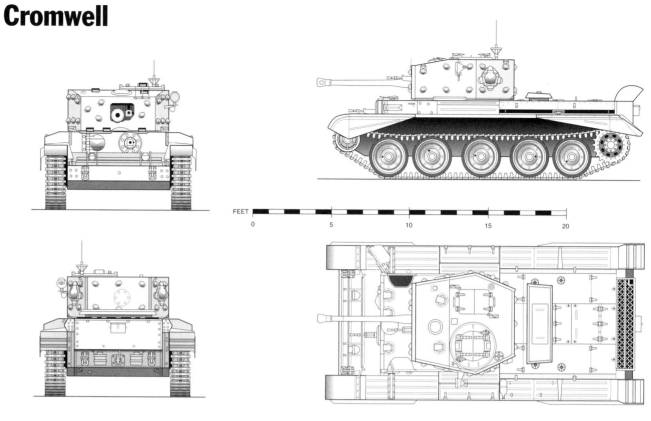

FEET
0   5   10   15   20

17-pdr Self-Propelled Valentine
Archer

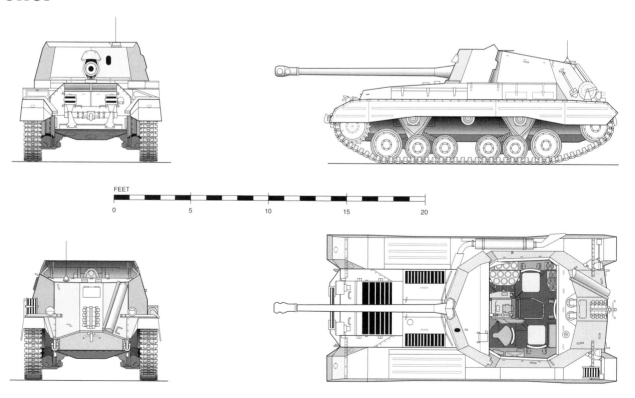

FEET
0   5   10   15   20

Churchill AVRE Carpet Layer Mk. II (Type C)

Fitted with Petard spigot mortar and deep-wading trunking.

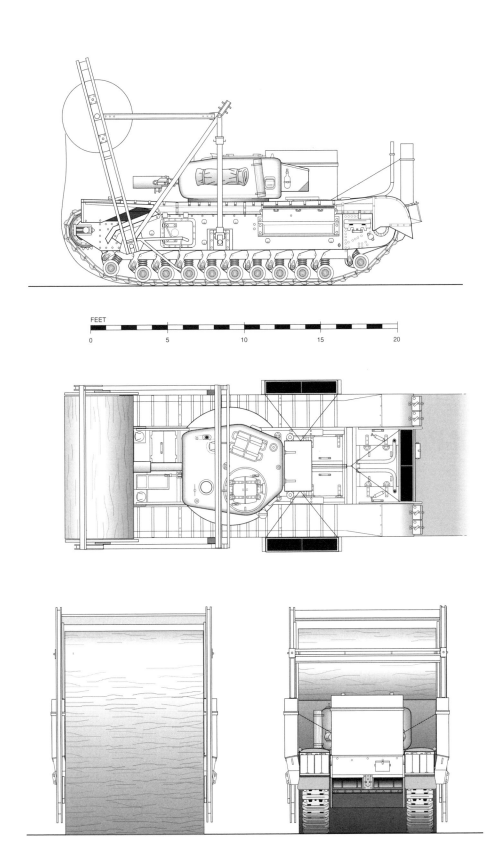

FEET

0   5   10   15   20

Anti-Aircraft Mk. II Cruiser Tank Crusader III

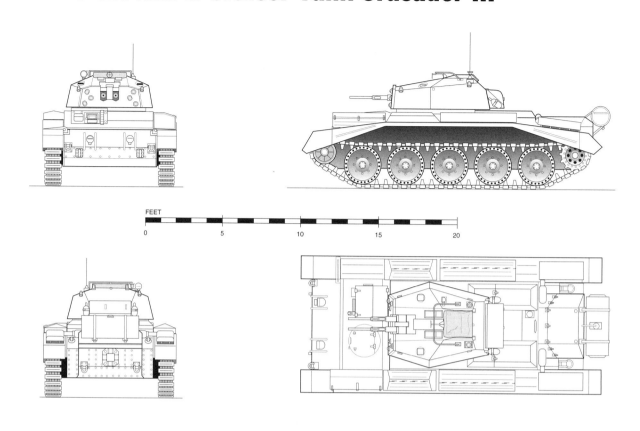

FEET

0   5   10   15   20

17-pdr Self-Propelled M10 Achilles IIC

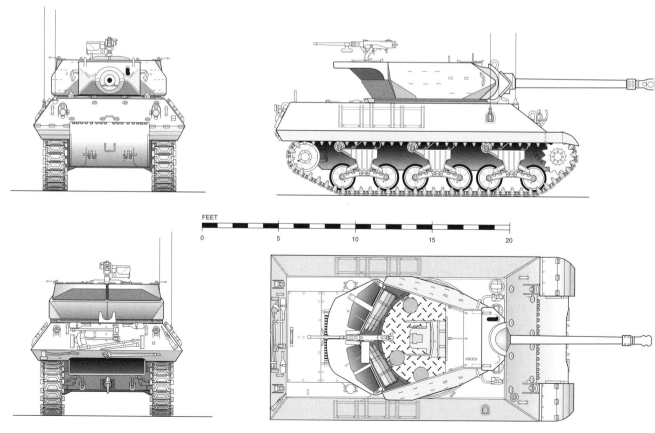

FEET

0   5   10   15   20

AEC Mk. I Armored Car

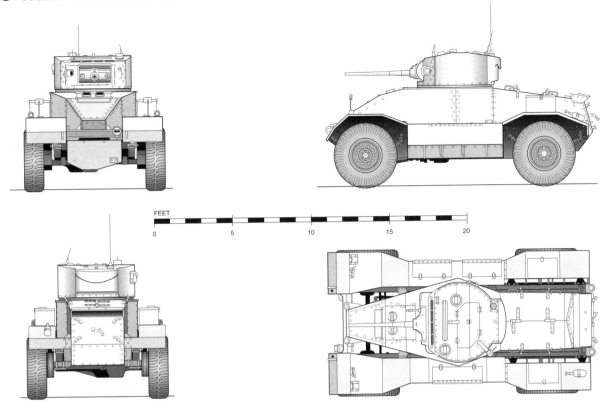

FEET
0   5   10   15   20

Grant Scorpion IV
Mine Clearing Flail

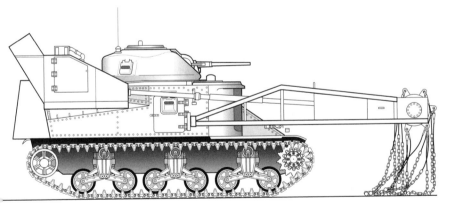

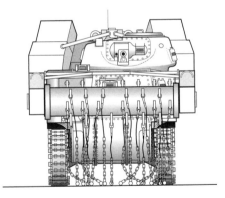

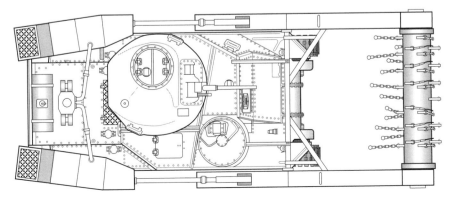

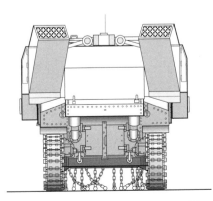

Sherman V Crab II Flail
Mine Clearance Device

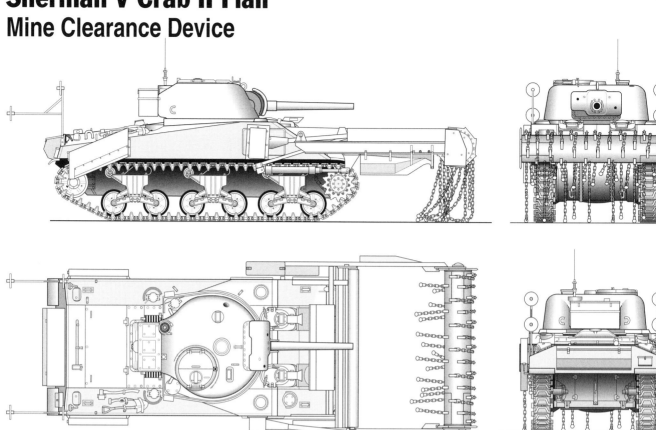

Challenger Cruiser Tank (A30)
Fitted with the 17-pdr gun.

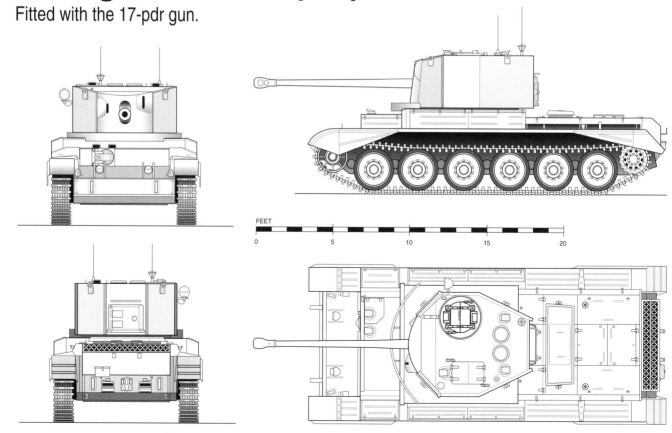

FEET

0   5   10   15   20

AEC Mk. III Armored Car

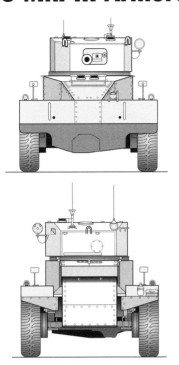
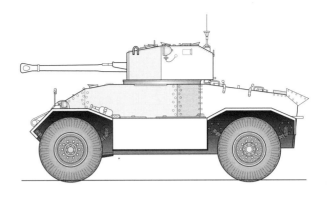
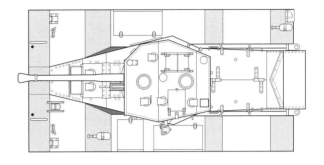

Churchill Mk. VII Crocodile Flamethrower

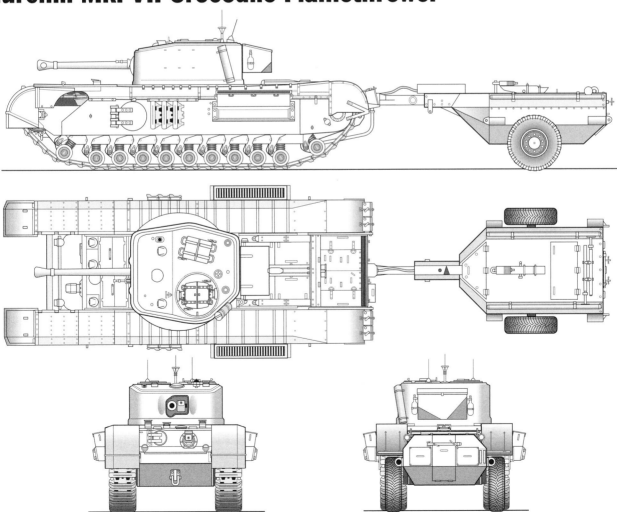

Sherman BARV (Beach Armored Recovery Vehicle)

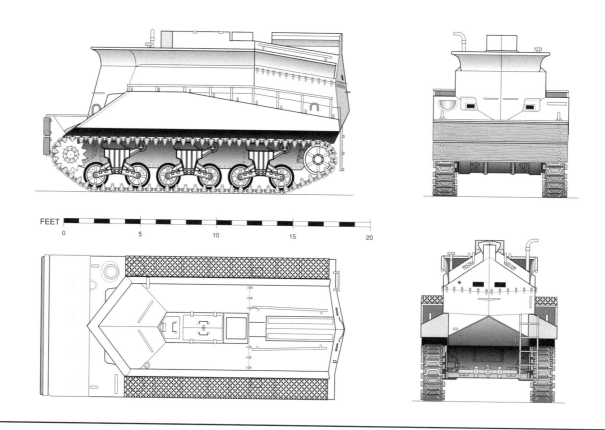

FEET
0   5   10   15   20

Humber Mk. II Armored Car

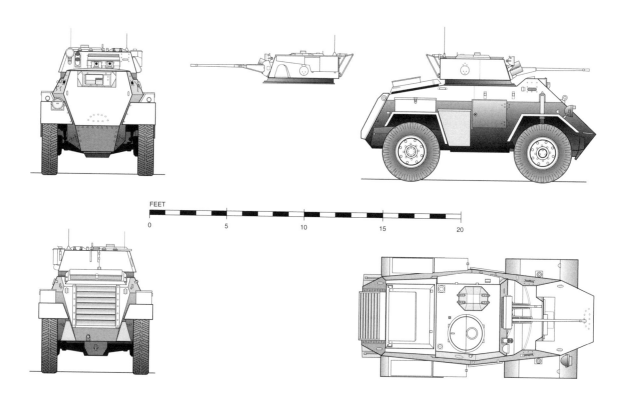

FEET
0   5   10   15   20

Morris Mk. II Reconnaissance Car

The earlier Morris Mk. I was a rear engined 4x2 rear wheel drive vehicle with a smooth enclosed underbelly that gave it quite good cross-country capability.

On the 4x4 wheeled Mk. II version, the coil springs were replaced with leaf springs. About 2,200 Morris Light Reconnaissance Cars, both Mk. I and Mk. II were built, including turretless OP versions.

Side view with roof hatches raised and the Boys anti-tank rifle in firing position.

FEET

0   5   10   15   20

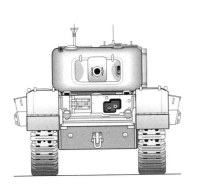

Inner Face

Aperture Closed

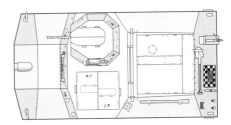

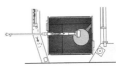

Top view of hatches up and Boys anti-tank rifle in firing position.

Churchill NA75 Infantry Tank
with 75mm Sherman gun

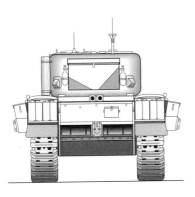

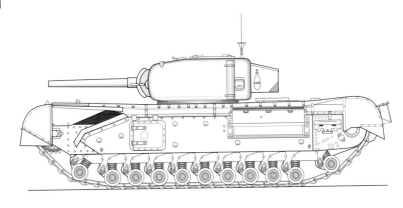

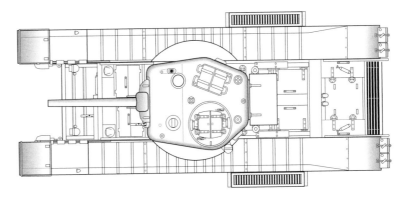

Mk. VII Light Tank Tetrarch
Fitted with Littlejohn adapter.

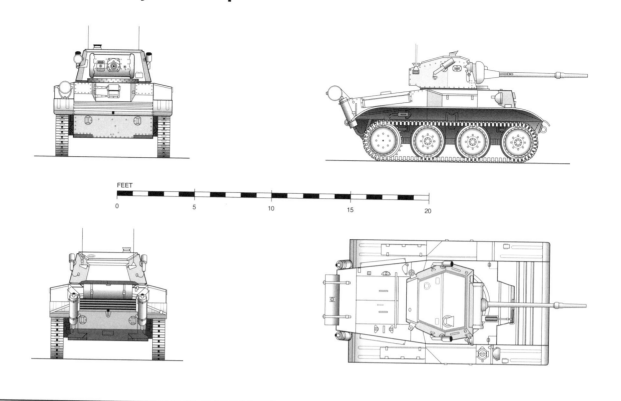

FEET

0   5   10   15   20

Sherman VC Firefly
17-pdr armed M4A4.

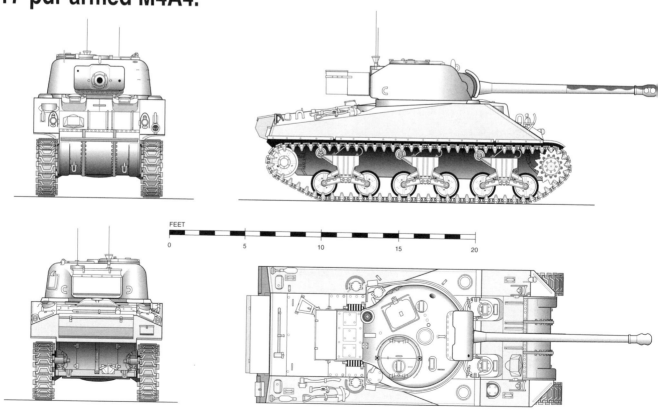

FEET

0   5   10   15   20

13A3 Stuart V Recce
n British, Canadian, and Polish service.

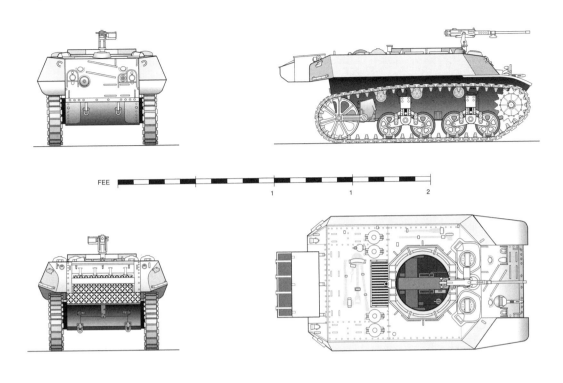

FEE

1   1   2

Sherman IC Firefly
17-pdr armed M4 hybrid.

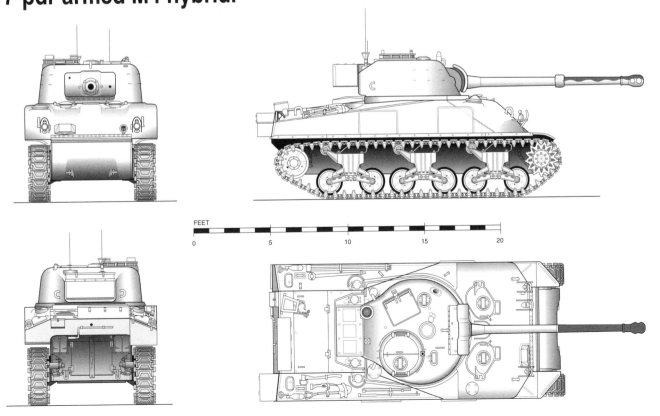

FEET

0   5   10   15   20

Mk. IV Infantry Tank (A22) Churchill Mk. V
With 95mm howitzer.

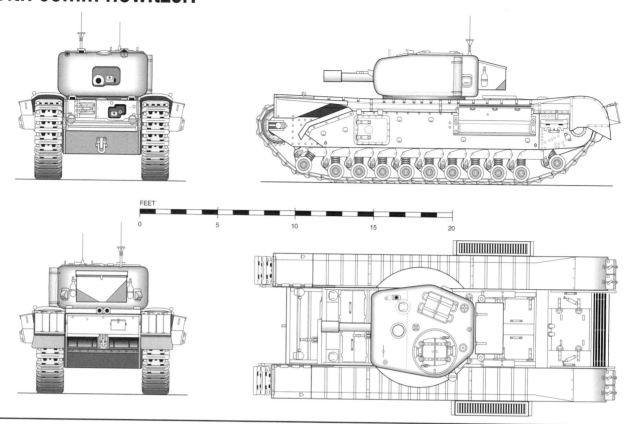

FEET

0   5   10   15   20

M3 CDL (Canal Defense Light)
On early M3 Medium Tank chassis.

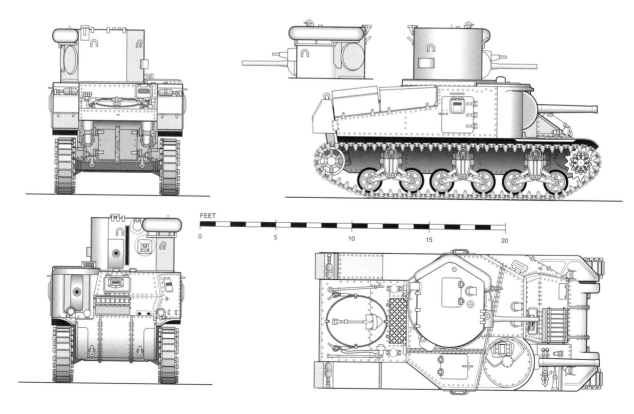

FEET

0   5   10   15   20

Mk. III Infantry Tank Valentine Mk. XI

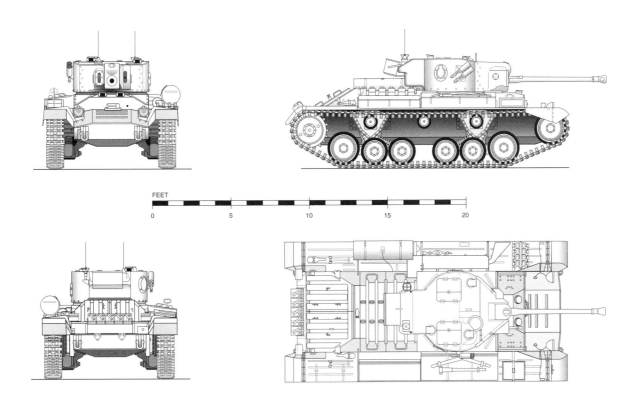

FEET

0   5   10   15   20

Comet Cruiser Tank (A34)
With 77mm shortened 17-pdr gun.

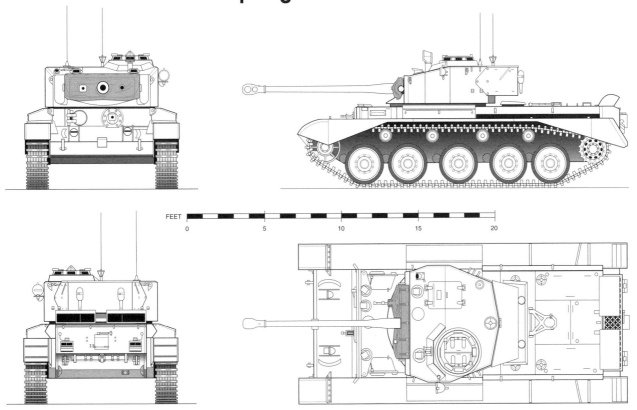

FEET

0   5   10   15   20

Churchill 3-inch Gun Carrier Mk. I (A22D)

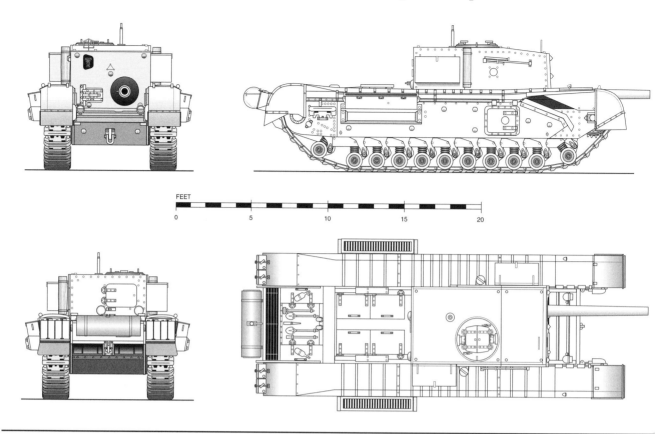

FEET

0 5 10 15 20

Avenger (A30)

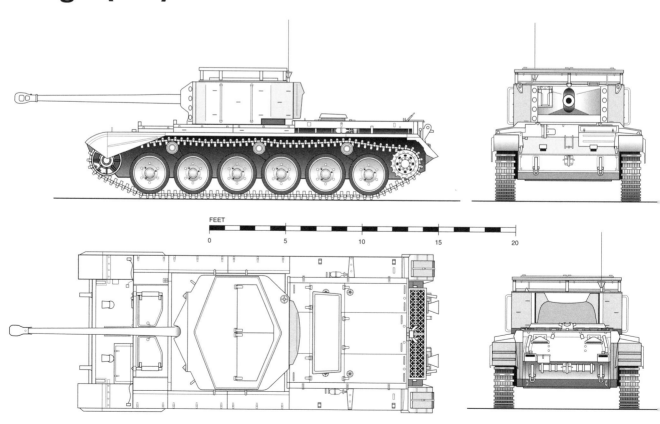

FEET

0 5 10 15 20

lack Prince Infantry Tank (A43)

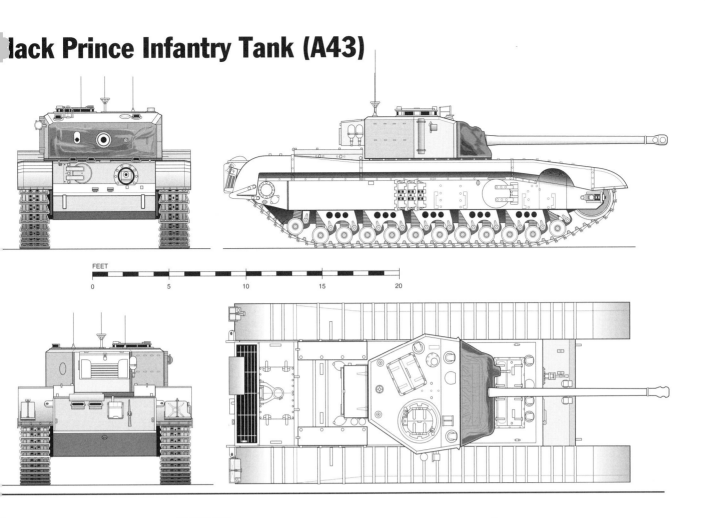

FEET
0   5   10   15   20

Centurion Mk. I MBT (A41 prototype pilot No. 2)

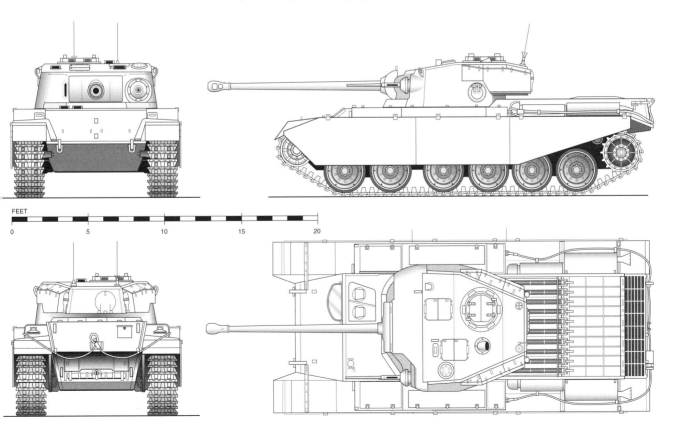

FEET
0   5   10   15   20

Tortoise Assault Tank (A39)

Mounting a 32-pdr gun, this project was begun in 1943, and six prototypes were finished by 1947.

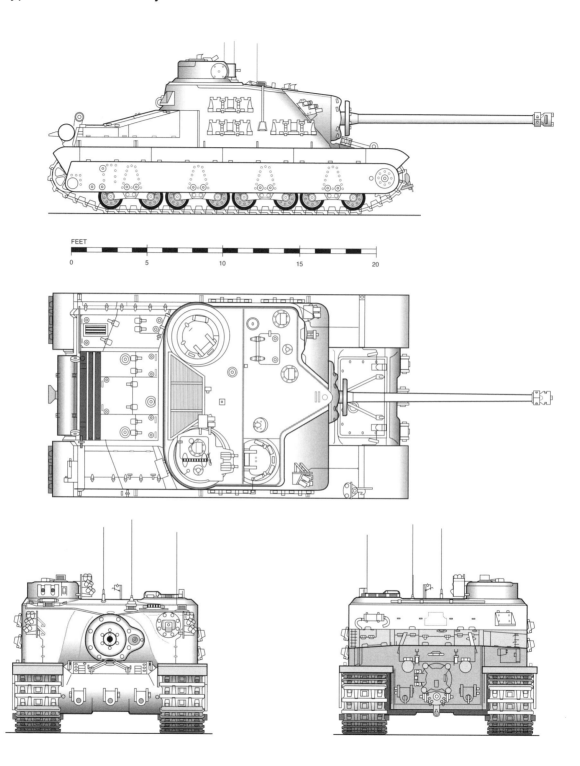

FEET

0   5   10   15   20

The Tortoise Heavy Assault Tank (A39) was a massive vehicle built along the same line of thinking as the German Jagdtiger. With a 32-pdr gun and 9 inches of frontal armor, it weighed in at 78 tons and had a speed of 12mph. Secondary armament consisted of three Besa machine guns, one in the hull front and two in a small rotating turret on the hull top.

CANADA

Ram I Cruiser Tank
Early version with 2-pdr gun.

In January 1941, Canada began development of its own tank design, using the lower hull and automotive components of the American M3 Medium, but with a new upper hull and armament that would meet British requirements. Casting of the hull and turret was initially done by General Steel Castings in the US, and later in Montreal. Final assembly took place at Montreal Locomotive Works, and the first Ram cruiser tanks started coming off the line in the summer of 1941.

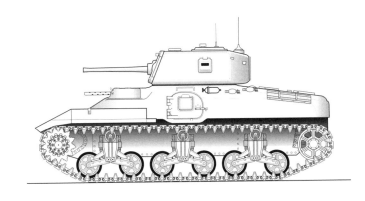

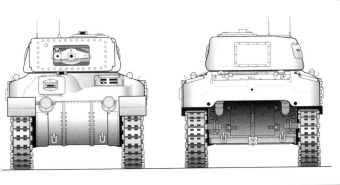

FEET 0 5 10 15 20

Ram II Cruiser Tank
Late version with 6-pdr gun.

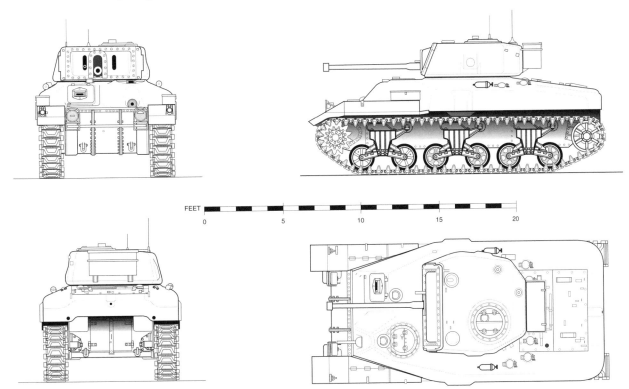

FEET 0 5 10 15 20

Grizzly I Cruiser Tank

Canadian-built M4A1

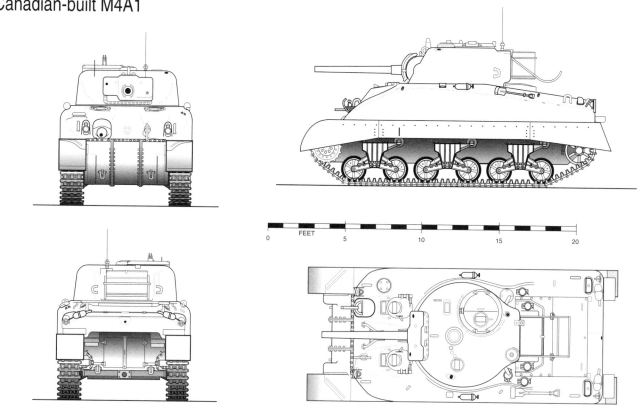

FEET

0   5   10   15   20

C15-TA Armored Truck

On 15 cwt, 4x4 truck chassis.

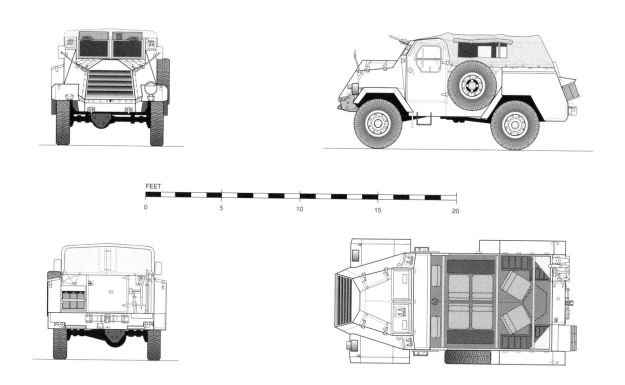

FEET

0   5   10   15   20

Otter Armored Car
Car Light Recon, G.M. Mk. I
Otter Mk. I

The Otter Light Recon was used mainly by reconnaissance regiments of the division and saw extensive use in Italy. It was also used by Canadian engineer bridging companies and also on convoy patrol as AA protection. Its armament consisted of one Bren light machine gun in the open turret and a Boys anti-tank rifle in the hull front.

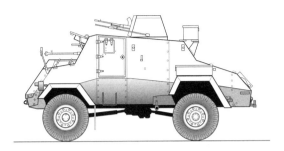

FEET
0   5   10   15   20

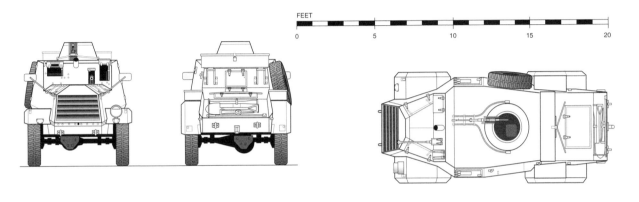

Sexton I Self-Propelled 25-pdr Gun
Early production of first 124 vehicles: S-15937 – CS-204821 variations.

Designed and built in Canada on the Ram chassis as a self-propelled mount for the British 25-pdr QF field gun. Production began in early 1943 and continued until 1945. Total production was 2,150, including Sexton II. The early Sextons were rushed into production and numerous changes followed. The first examples were fitted with a total of 8 different track types. Shown here are the T-54E1 steel chevron tracks. Many of these first 125 were later retrofitted with the heavy-duty trailing idler bogies as used on the Sexton II.

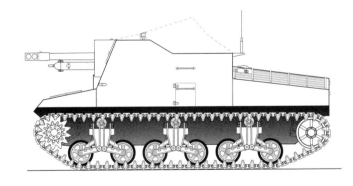

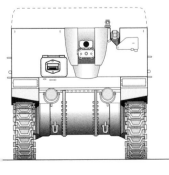

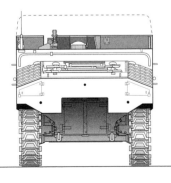

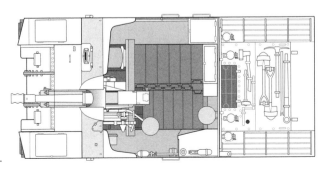

CMP Bofors Self-Propelled Anti-Aircraft Gun
(CMP Ford F60B 40mm Bofors S.P.)

In Canadian Army service 1944–45.

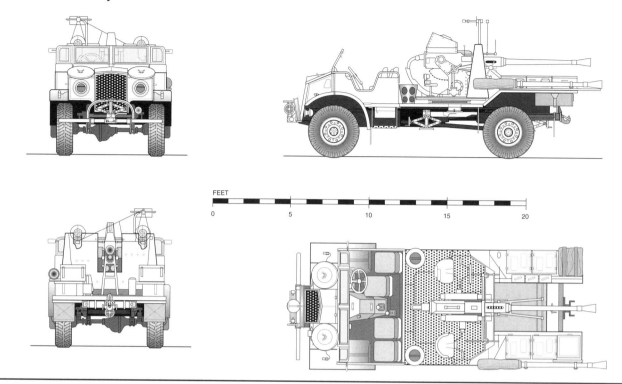

FEET

0   5   10   15   20

Ford Lynx Scout Cars I & II

These scout cars were used for short-range recon by armored regiments, armored car regiments, Royal Canadian Corps of Signals in armored formations, and recon regiment HQs, among others.

FEET

0   5   10   15   20

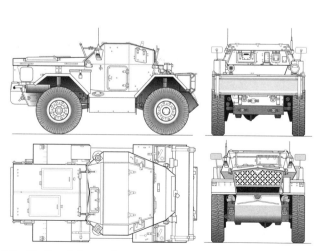

Mk. III, Ford, Lynx I
Lynx I displays the rear air intake grille, folding plate cabin roof, and early stowage bin arrangement. Many of these early Ford Lynx Scout Cars were eventually upgraded to the Lynx II standard by means of a modification kit.

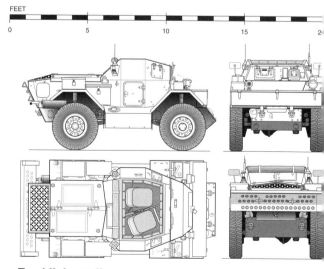

Ford II, Lynx II
Lynx II showing the new topside air intake grille, open-topped cabin, and final stowage bin arrangement. The interior arrangement of the Lynx I was basically identical to that of the Lynx II shown here.

Fox Armored Car (G.M.)
Mk. I, Fox I

The Fox Armored Car was the first attempt by General Motors of Canada to produce a rear-engined vehicle. The design reflected the British Humber Mk. III but was redesigned to use Canadian components. The chassis was based on the CMP Chevrolet CGT Field Artillery tractor, and the basic hull and turret were built by the Hamilton Bridge Company. A total of 1,116 vehicles, with the first 330 running on Runflat tires. The Fox was used by the divisional reconnaissance regiment of 1st Canadian Infantry in Italy during 1944. Few, if any, saw action in Northwest Europe.

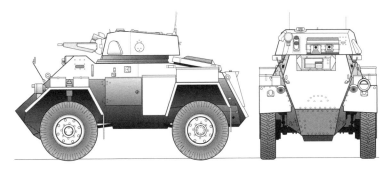

FEET
0   5   10   15   20

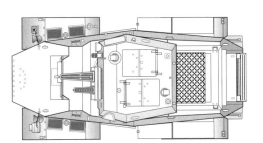

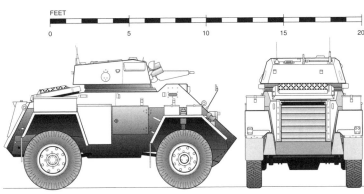

Sexton II Self-Propelled 25-pdr Gun
Late production of 1,436 vehicles: S-233626 – S-235061 inclusive.

After endless detail changes, the production series was more or less finalized at vehicle 125 and became Sexton II. The 3-piece transmission housing appears to have lingered until 474. Track types appear to have varied dramatically. The most obvious recognition features are the batteries and auxilliary generator boxes with their accompanying water can holders on either side at the rear. Canadian Dry Pin track and heavy-duty suspension with trailing idlers also depict the Sexton II.

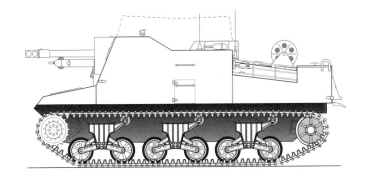

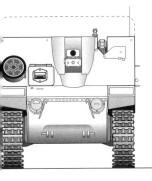

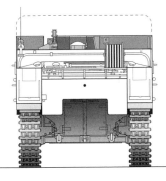

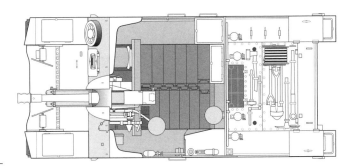

Ram Badger Flamethrower Tank

Late-production Ram II chassis and suspension, fitted with Wasp II flame gun.

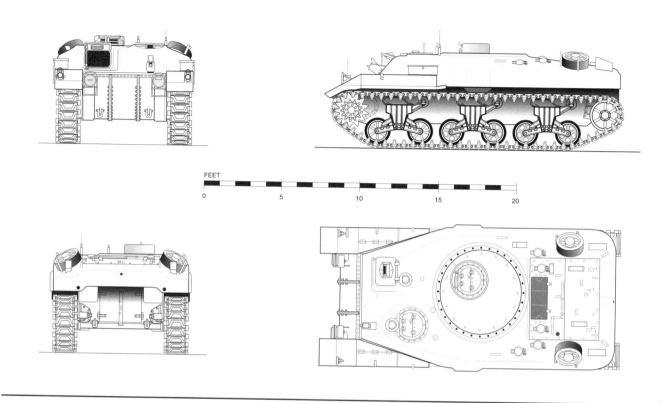

RM Kangaroo Armored Personnel Carrier

Late-production Ram II chassis and suspension.

The Canadian Kangaroo was the first fully tracked armored personnel carrier (APC). The version shown here used the Canadian Ram tank chassis, minus the turret. Other Kangaroos were based on the M7 Priest with gun removed and armor plate added. Devised by Lt. Gen. Simonds during the early battles in Europe, the intent was to give his infantry the speed and protection required to stay abreast of the tanks as they advanced.

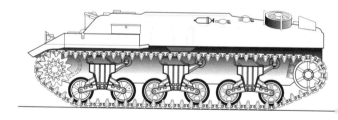

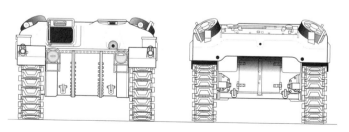

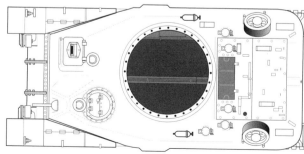

Chevrolet Field Artillery Tractor

The standard Field Artillery Tractor was based on the 3-ton 101-inch wheelbase chassis, with a number of different cab styles. Ford and General Motors in Canada built more than 12,000 of this series during the war. They were often used to tow the 25-pdr with its platform stowed under the gun trail and an artillery trailer between.

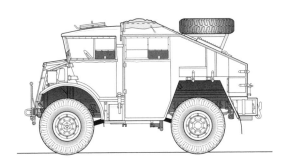

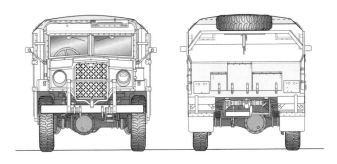

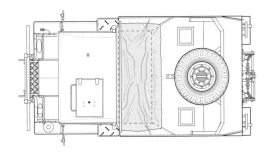

Windsor Carrier
Late-production model.

By 1943, the Canadian Universal Carrier design was deemed to be underpowered and renowned for its pitching motion. This new design was meant to solve these problems and fulfill five separate tasks: 6-pdr towing, senior commander vehicle, junior commander vehicle, mortar carrier, and 6-pdr ammunition carrier.

The Windsor Carrier was powered by a 96hp V-8 engine driving through a standard clutch, 4-speed transmission, drive shaft, and 2-speed rear axle to the drive sprockets. The suspension was elongated to accommodate two full bogie assemblies fitted with trackguide return rollers, and the springs on the four bogies absorbed all road shocks.

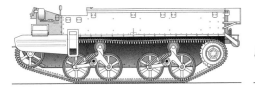

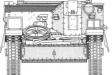

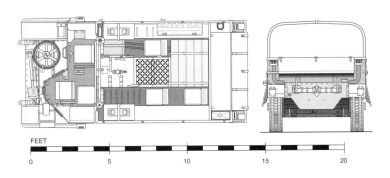

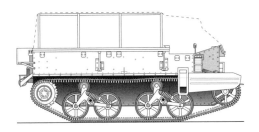

FEET

0   5   10   15   20

Skink 20mm Quad Anti-Aircraft Tank
On the Canadian-built Grizzly Cruiser Tank.

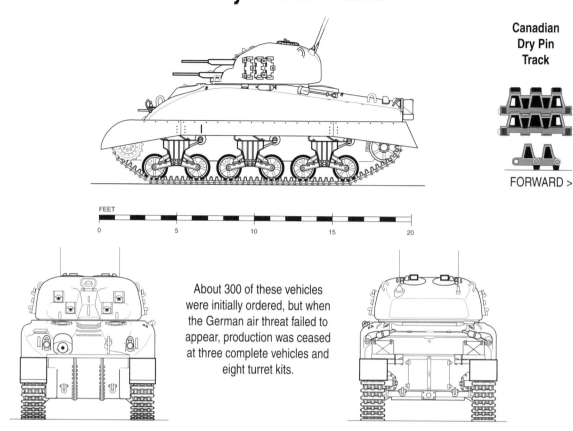

Canadian Dry Pin Track

FORWARD >

FEET

0   5   10   15   20

About 300 of these vehicles were initially ordered, but when the German air threat failed to appear, production was ceased at three complete vehicles and eight turret kits.

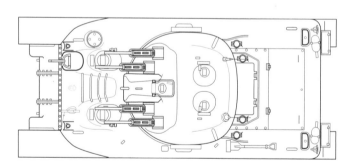

The turret castings were prepared by Dominion Steel & Foundries of Hamilton, Ontario, in late 1943. Earlier that year, Waterloo Manufacturing Co. of Kitchener-Waterloo, Ontario, had designed a pilot turret with the Hispano-Suiza 20mm guns in position. However, once the turret assembly was well along, Montgomery prohibited the use of the Hispano-Suiza guns in 21st Army Group, insisting that old Oerlikon 20mm ammunition be used. This threw a wrench into the production schedule that likely killed the whole project. It had to be totally refitted with Quad Polsten guns, and turret redesign began again in February 1944. This all led to eventual cancellation of the project after only three had been completed.

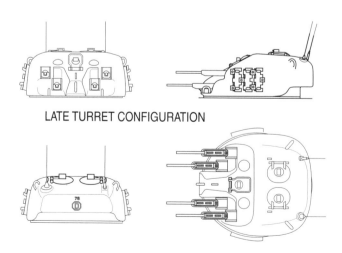

LATE TURRET CONFIGURATION

FCM Char 2C Heavy Tank

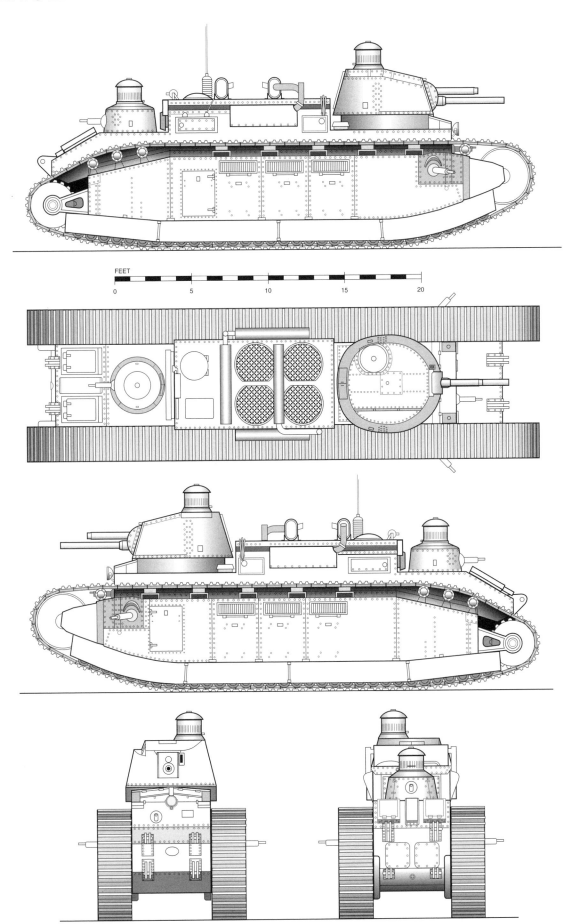

FEET

0   5   10   15   20

AMD Laffly S.15 TOE Armored Car
In service from 1934 to 1942.

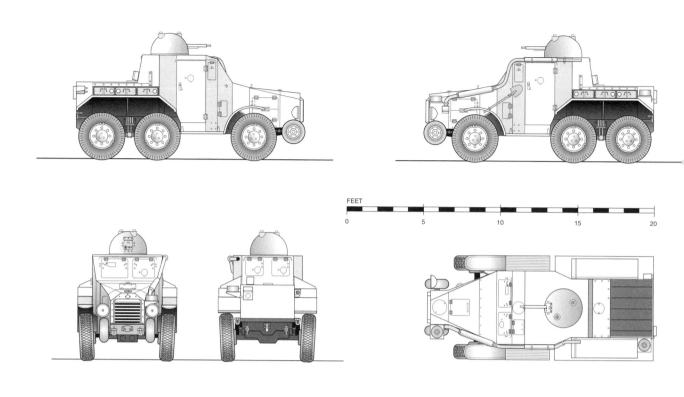

AMC Schneider P16 (M29)
Citroën-Kégresse half-tracked armored car.

During the 1930s, the AMC Schneider P16 appears to have served in six of the French Cavalry's seven "Groupes Autonomes d'autos-mitrailleuses" (GAAM) then in existence. However, they were never quite satisfactory and were replaced by the Panhard 178 armored cars and Hotchkiss H-35 and H-38 tanks, once these were available.

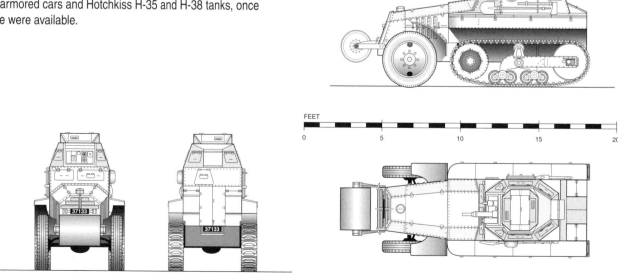

har Renault D2
Vith SA34 47mm gun

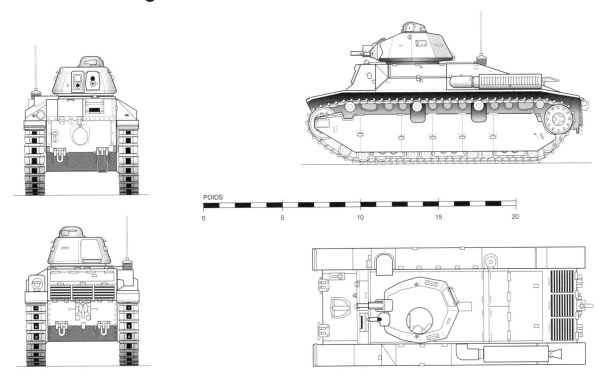

POIDS

0   5   10   15   20

affly Type W15 TCC
Chasseur de chars (47mm modèle 1937 gun)

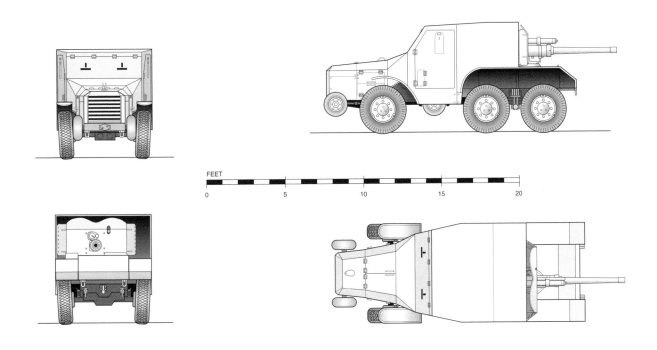

FEET

0   5   10   15   20

Char B1 bis Medium Tank (Renault 1936)
APX 4 turret

The Char de bataille B1 bis was France's main battle tank in 1940. As an improved version of the Char B1, it was now fitted with the new APX 4 turret mounting a 47mm gun, along with a 75mm gun in the bow. Numerous French firms were involved in its production, including Renault, Schneider, FAMH St-Chammond, and FCM, with ARL overseeing development.

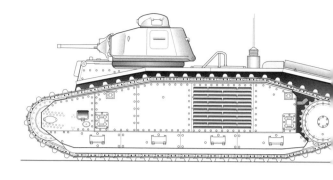

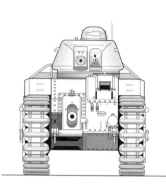

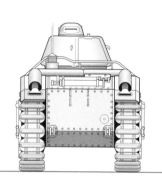

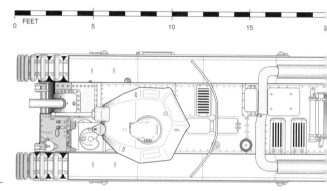

FEET
0   5   10   15

FCM 36 Light Tank (Char lèger Modèle 1936 FCM)

Ordered by the French Army in 1936, this light tank was somewhat unique for the times because of its rakish angled armor and the use of a diesel engine. By 1939, about 100 had been delivered. It mounted a 37mm cannon and had a two-man crew. The FCM 36 was deployed during the 1940 French campaign but met the same fate as most other French armor at that time. The surviving vehicles were later utilized as chassis for several German self-propelled guns.

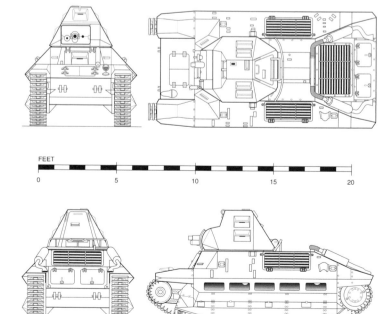

FEET
0   5   10   15   20

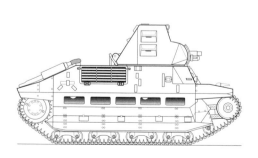

AMC Renault ACG 1
Light Tank (1935 type)

The AMC 35 was built by Renault and made use of a bell-crank scissors suspension with horizontal rubber springing. The hull was of riveted construction using rolled steel plate. The running-gear included on each side five road-wheels, a front sprocket drive wheel, a back idler, and five return rollers. The maximum armor was 25mm, and the AMC 35 had a combat weight of approximately 15 tons, but its petrol consumption was catastrophic. Thus, the AMC 35 was limited to 3/4 of an hour of range on any terrain. The running-gear was in fact badly adapted for the speed of this tank and caused this excessive consumption. Very few were built, some with 25mm guns and later with 47mm as shown here.

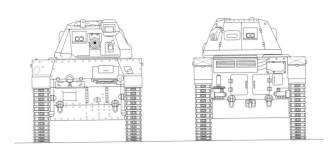

AMD Laffly 80 AM Laffly-Vincennes
Reconnaissance Car (Automitrailleuse de Découverte)

The final design was based on the 1917 White-Laffly AM, and this car was in service by 1935. Based on the Laffly LC2 truck chassis, it was considered already obsolete as it came off the production line. Production was halted at 28 vehicles, but these few soldiered on right into World War II and beyond, several showing up in Algeria as late as 1955. The initial armament was one 13.2mm Hotchkiss heavy machine gun and one 7.5mm light machine gun.

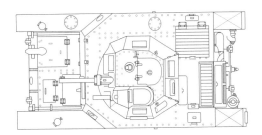

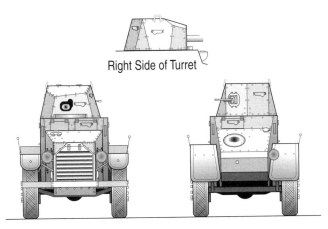

Right Side of Turret

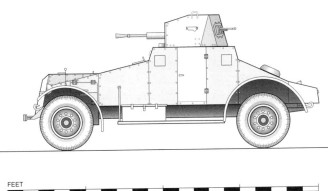

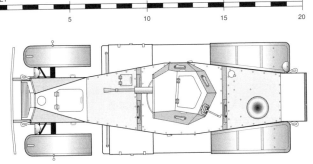

AMD Panhard 178
Armored Car (Modèle 1935)

The Panhard Model 1935 was mainly used in a reconnaissance role with both the French infantry and cavalry units. They took part in both the first stages of war on the French border with Germany in 1939–40 and the eventual invasion.

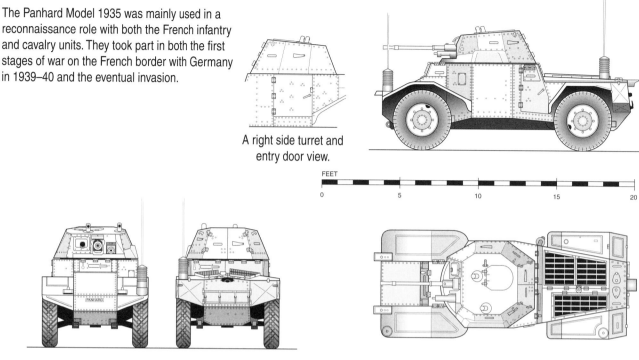

A right side turret and entry door view.

FEET

0   5   10   15   20

Lorraine 1938L
Le véhicle blindé de chasseurs portés (Armored Personnel Carrie

These vehicles were developed by the company Société Lorraine in an attempt to fill a requirement by the French Army for a vehicle to replace their Type UE chenillettes with a larger, more practical all-purpose carrier.

The original Lorraine 37L was accepted and went into production in 1937, with an initial order for 214 vehicles. This supply vehicle version was the only type in mass production at the time of the German invasion. Eventually, 432 chassis were produced for all types.

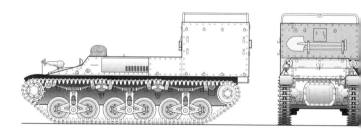

FEET

0   5   10   15

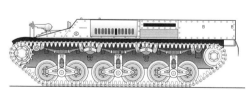

Type 37 L Supply Vehicle
(Tracteur de ravitaillement pour chars 1937 L)

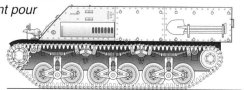

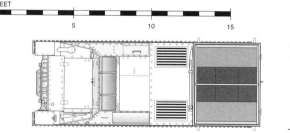

Type 1939 model APC design
In 1939, Lorraine built a prototype of an even more practica APC, which was well advanced for the time, but the war intervened before it could go into serious production.

AMD Panhard 178B

The Panhard 178B was basically a postwar vehicle. Late [in] World War II, the French began to fit their Panhard [1]78 with a new and much larger cast and welded turret. [T]his increased the vehicle weight by 500 pounds but did [n]ot seem to affect mobitily. The turret now mounted a [4]7mm cannon and a coaxial 7.5mm machine gun.

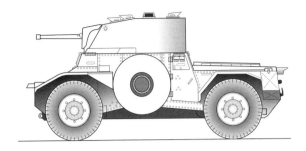

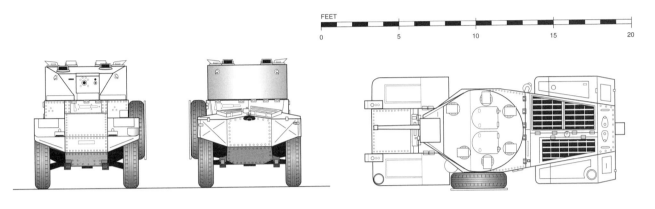

SOMUA S-35 Medium Tank

One of the best AFVs of its day, the type was known as the SOMUA S-35 to most of Europe, though to the French Army, it was the Automitrailleuse de Combat (AMC) modèle 1935 SOMUA. The S-35 had many features that would later become standard. The hull and turret were both cast components at a time when most contemporary tanks used riveted plates. The cast armor was not only well shaped for extra protection, but it was also much thicker than the norm for the time. For all that, it still had a good reserve of power provided by a V-8 petrol engine for lively battlefield performance, and a good operational radius of action was ensured by large internal fuel tanks. The S-35 was armed with a powerful gun: the 47mm SA35 was one of the most powerful weapons of the day and a gun that could still be regarded as a useful weapon in 1944. The secondary armament was a single 7.5mm (0.295-in) coaxial machine gun.

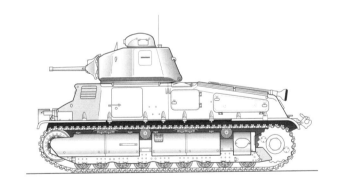

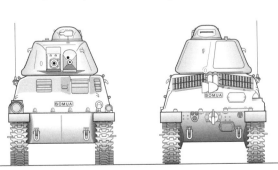

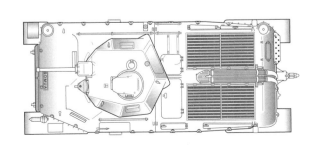

Renault R-35 Light Tank
Char léger Mle 1935 R

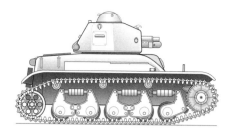

By 1940, the R-35 was the most numerous French tank in service, with more than 1,600 being built. A number were also exported to Romania (40), Turkey (100), Poland (50), and Yugoslavia (50). It was classified as a light tank but had armor heavy enough to act as infantry support. The cast hull was made of three pieces, plus a steel plate underpan. The standard APX-R turret was fitted with a 37mm SA 18 gun (semi-automatic, model 1918) very similar to that mounted in the earlier FT-17. Around 1938, some were fitted with unditching tails. They were normally issued to independent tank battalions assigned to support infantry divisions. The Germans managed to acquire about 870 of them from various sources early in the war, and they ended up on all fronts and in many configurations.

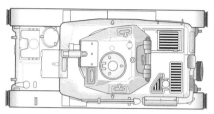

Showing the re hatch in the op position.

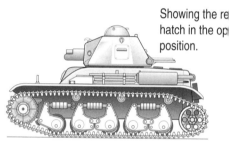

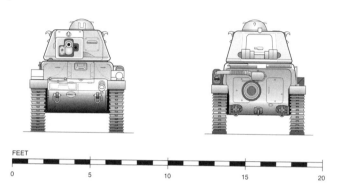

FEET

0   5   10   15   20

Hotchkiss H-39 Light Tank Char léger Mle 1939 H
Mounting the long 37mm SA 38 cannon

The H-35 light tank was in full production when it was realized that it was underpowered, and plans for a revised model with a more powerful engine soon emerged. The old 75hp engine was replaced by a 125hp Hotchkiss 6-cylinder version, and this altered the rear deck considerably. The latest APX-R turret was fitted, and this model also featured the new steel-rimmed roadwheels, as opposed to the earlier rubber-rimmed type. By 1939, the SA 38 long-barreled version of the 37mm gun was available and began replacing the short SA 18 cannon on many H-39s. The H-39 chassis saw service with the German occupying forces, and 72 of them were shipped to the Becker firm in Krefeld for conversion to self-propelled guns.

This shows the early SA 18 short 37mm turret.

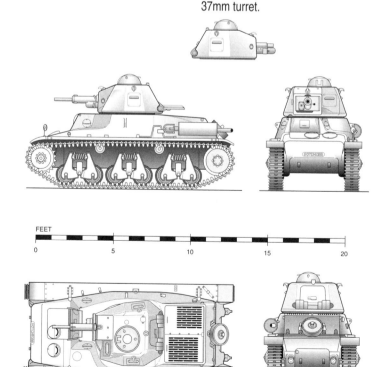

FEET

0   5   10   15   20

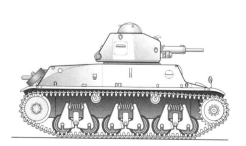

BT-5 Fast Tank (Bystrochodnyj)
Model 1934 Fast Tank, standard production turret.

The BT series of "Fast Tanks" was mainly assigned to independent tank brigades or in support of cavalry units. They were based on the Christie M1930 convertible tank, which had been rejected by the US Army. One of the main improvements that appeared on the BT-5 was a pair of good-sized twin hatches in the turret roof and an added bustle. The stowage system was also much improved. There were also numeous variants of the BT-5, from flamethrower to artillery versions, much like the various T-26 models.

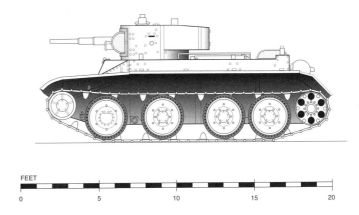

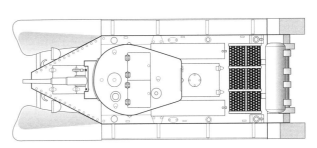

FEET

0   5   10   15   20

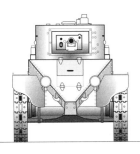
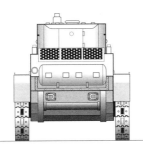

BT-7 Fast Tank
(Model 1937)

Concern about riveted tanks led to a redesign on the BT-5, and the BT-7 Model 1935 was the result. It now sported a welded turret, along with a redesigned and rounded front end for the hull. At the rear, the muffler was now completely enclosed. In 1937, sloped sides appeared on the turret to help increase ballistic protection.

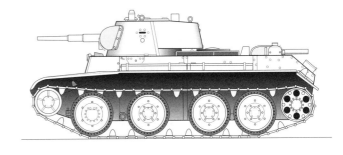

FEET

0   5   10   15   20

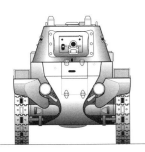
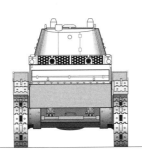
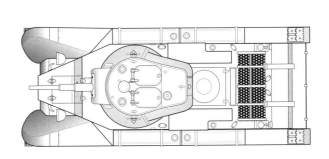

BA-10M (Model 1939)
Medium Armored Car

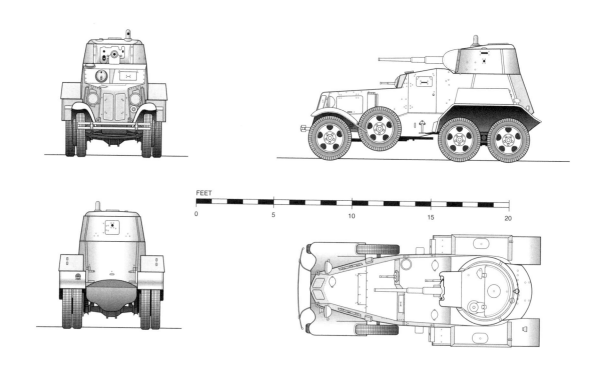

T-26S (Model 1939)
Light Tank

The T-26S Model 1937 was an upgraded version of the Model 1933, with a sleeker turret design and better armor, increasing the weight to 10.5 tons. The gun was also stabilzed for better accuracy. The Model 1939 featured a cast or drop-forged gun mantlet. The upper superstructure was also redesigned with wider and better angled side panels, allowing increased fuel and ammunition stowage.

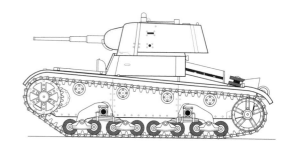

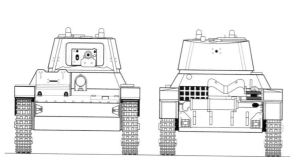

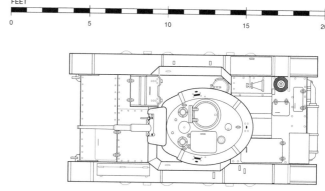

SMK Heavy Tank (1939)
(Sergei Mironovich Kirov)

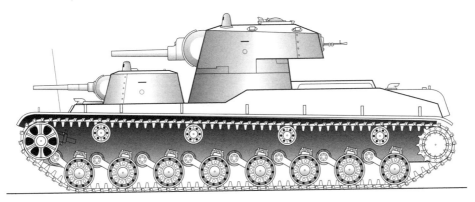

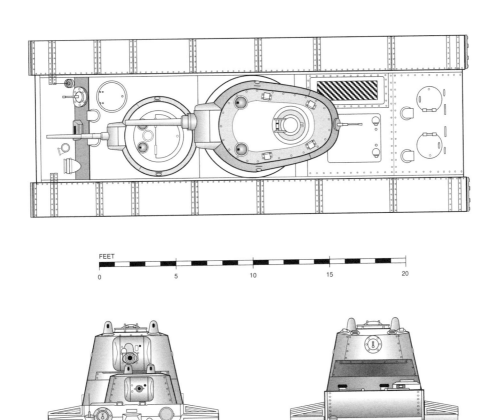

The 1930s had seen its share of multi-turreted super-heavy tanks, and the Russian SMK was among the largest of these. In April 1939, the nearly finished SMK rolled out of the Kirov Plant in Leningrad. Later that summer, it was shipped to the Kubinka Proving Grounds north of Moscow, and by September 1939, it was demonstrated to representatives of the Communist Party. By December, a decision had been made to send it to the Finnish Front in order to continue trials under real combat conditions. Fitted out with a crew of seven, the SMK now had 1,642 km under its belt and eventually travelled by rail to the Karelian Pass. Here it joined other heavy tanks as part of a special heavy tank company of 91st Tank Battalion.

The SMK took part in the assault on the Finnish fortifications near Summa but was soon immobilized and abandoned by its crew. It remained in place there for several months, and the Finns tried to tow it away but had nothing powerful enough to move it. The Russians also had trouble trying to recover it the following spring, and eventually, it was disassembled and shipped to Leningrad, where they decided to drop the project altogether.

T-28 Medium Tank (Model 1934)

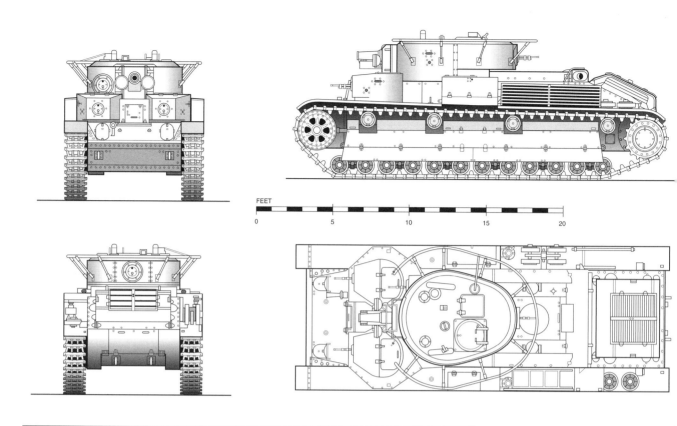

T-38 (Model 1937)
Light Amphibious Tank

The T-37 was given such an extensive redesign that it was soon designated the T-38 in 1936. The T-38 was wider and lower than the T-37, with better swimming capabilities. However, it was still driven by the GAZ-AA lorry engine and power train.

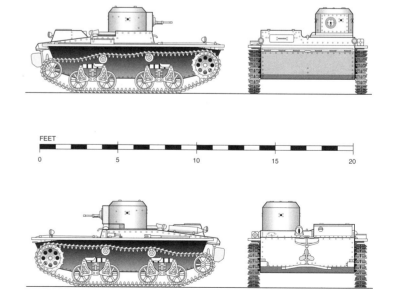

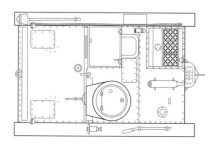

-35 (Model 1935)
Heavy Tank

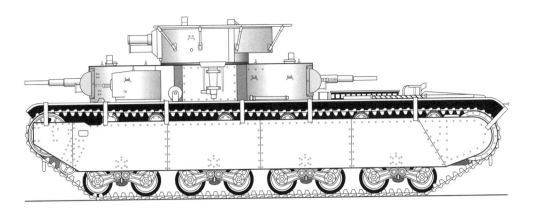

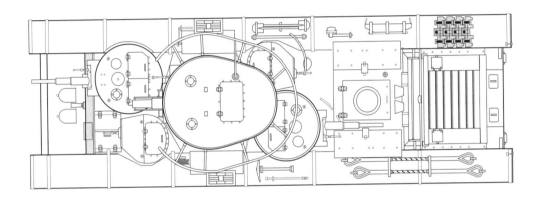

FEET

0   5   10   15   20

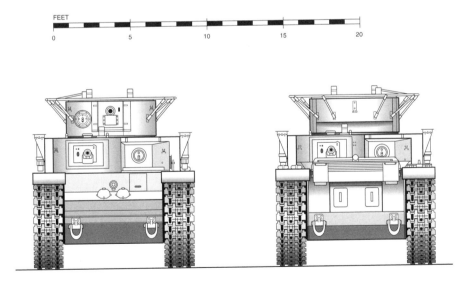

Design of the T-35 appears to have been influenced by the British Vickers Independent. This Russian version had a 76.2mm gun in the main turret and four sub-turrets, two with 37mm guns (later replaced with 45mm) and two with machine guns. Production began in 1933 with ten, and then about 35 were built in the 1935–38 period, and later, six improved versions were built with angled side armor on the turrets. In the end, there were about 61 built of all types.

KV-2 Heavy Tank (Model 1939)
Early

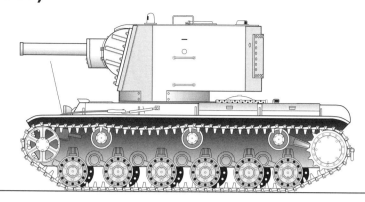
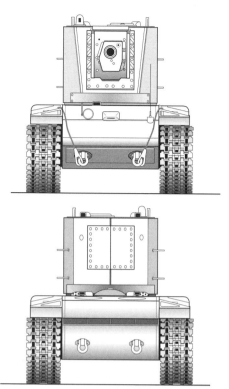

T-34 Medium Tank (Model 1940)
Initial production with L-11 gun and welded turret

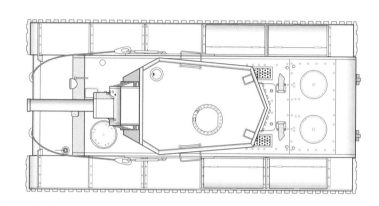
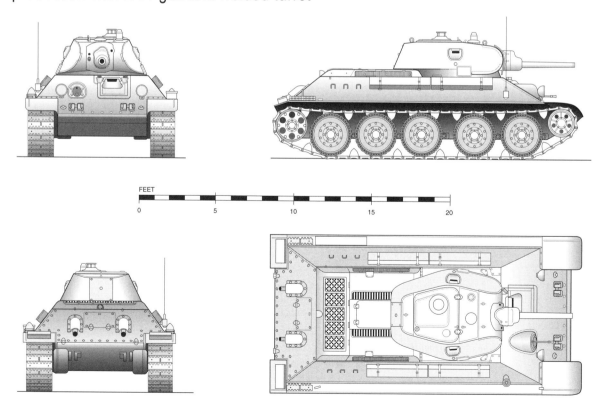

FEET

0   5   10   15   20

KV-2 Heavy Tank late (Model 1940)

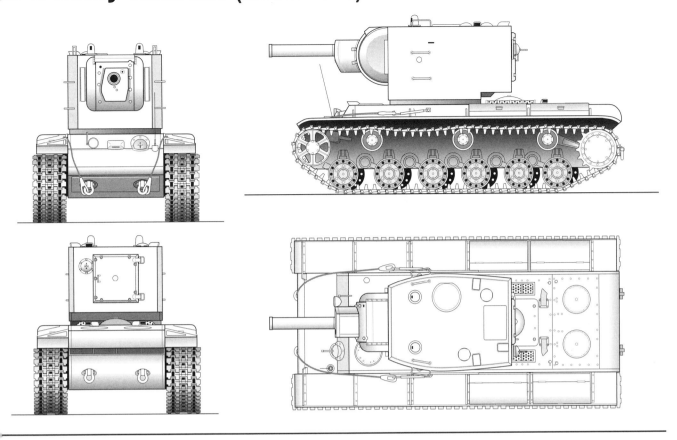

KV-1 Heavy Tank (Model 1941) welded turret

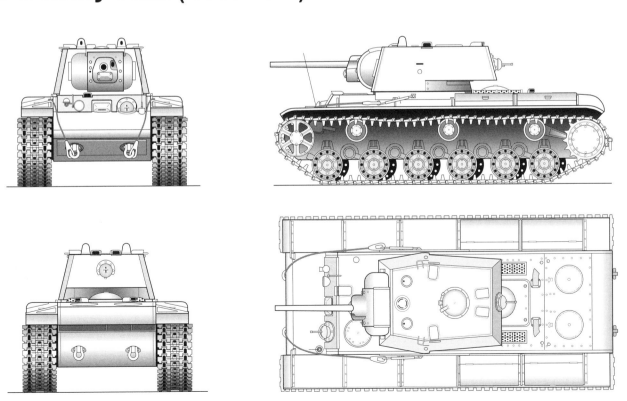

T-40 Amphibious Light Tank (Model 1940)

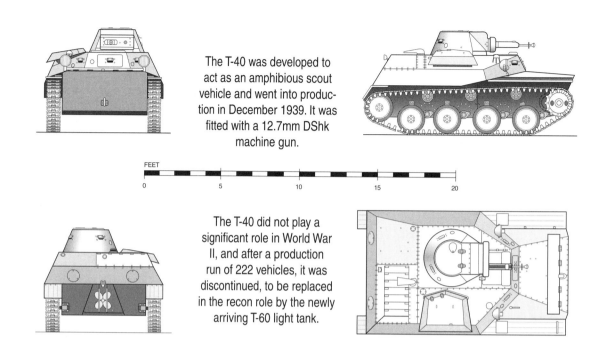

The T-40 was developed to act as an amphibious scout vehicle and went into production in December 1939. It was fitted with a 12.7mm DShk machine gun.

FEET

0   5   10   15   20

The T-40 did not play a significant role in World War II, and after a production run of 222 vehicles, it was discontinued, to be replaced in the recon role by the newly arriving T-60 light tank.

BA-6 Medium Armored Car (Model 1938)

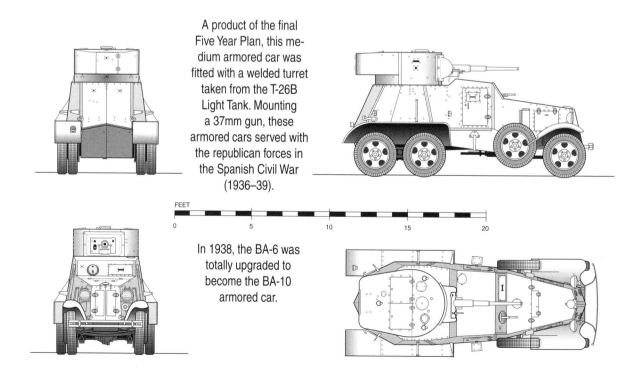

A product of the final Five Year Plan, this medium armored car was fitted with a welded turret taken from the T-26B Light Tank. Mounting a 37mm gun, these armored cars served with the republican forces in the Spanish Civil War (1936–39).

FEET

0   5   10   15   20

In 1938, the BA-6 was totally upgraded to become the BA-10 armored car.

KV-1 Heavy Tank (Model 1941)
Cast turret

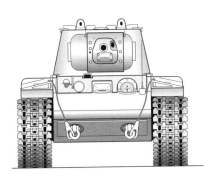

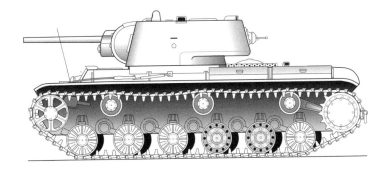

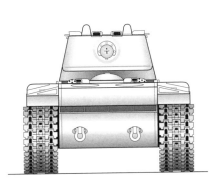

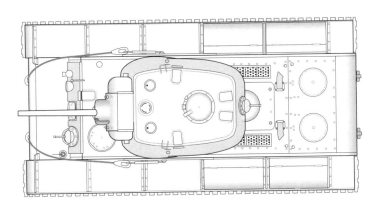

T-60 Light Tank (Model 1941)

When World War II began, the Soviets had small numbers of their new T-40 amphibious scout tank available for recon roles, and the T-60 was just coming into production. By September 41, the T-60 was acknowledged as the main Russian light tank and began to replace the vehicles lost in the early fighting. The early version featured spoked wheels and rear idlers, but the later Model 1942 went over to the simpler solid-disc type shown to the right. Otherwise, they were almost identical. Unfortunately, it mounted a TNsh 20mm gun, which was far from effective on the battlefield.

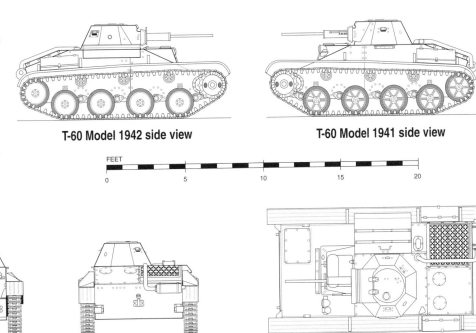

T-60 Model 1942 side view

T-60 Model 1941 side view

FEET

0   5   10   15   20

KV-220 Superheavy Tank
Prototype fitted with a 107mm gun
KV-3 (Object 220)

FEET

0   5   10   15   20

Komsomolyets STZ-3
Armored Artillery Tractor

The petite STZ-3 was introduced as an artillery tractor between 1938 and 1940. It was designed to tow the 45mm anti-tank gun crew and limbers for motorized units. There was also a fuel-carrying version with a large container replacing the seating area, which was intended to refuel tanks in the field. The artillery version was available during the Russo-Finnish War, and the Finns captured a goodly number of them to serve their own purposes. It also saw action at the beginning of World War II, but once it was obvious that the Russian 45mm anti-tank gun was obsolete, they were relegated to other purposes.

The bottom two drawings show the canvas cover raised over the seating area to protect the gun crew during inclement weather.

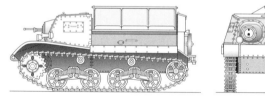

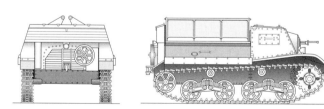

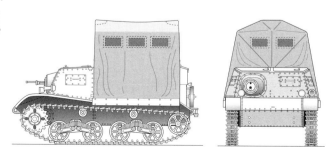

FEET

0   5   10   15   20

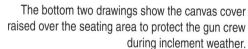

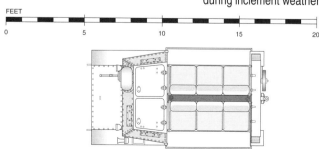

T-34/76 Medium Tank (Model 1942/43)
Late 1942 production with hard-edge turret

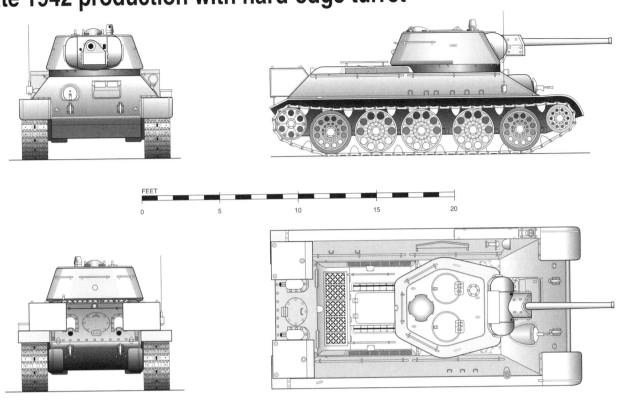

FEET

0   5   10   15   20

KV-1s Ekranami Heavy Tank (Model 1941)
With bolted-on appliqué armor and F-32 gun

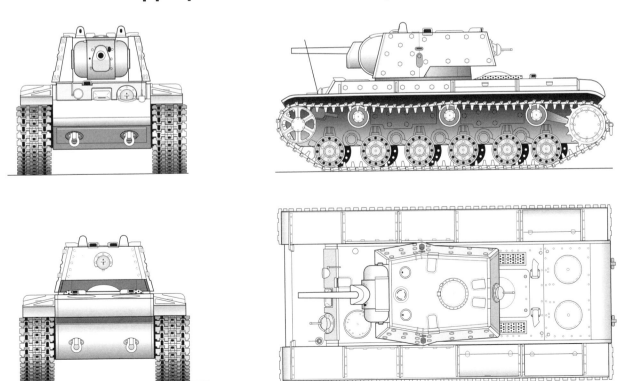

BA-64B Light Armored Car (Model 1943)

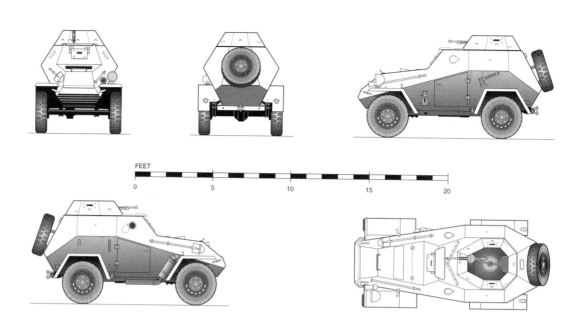

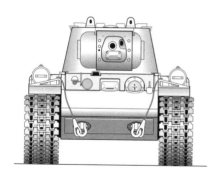

KV-1C Heavy Tank (Model 1942)
With ZiS-5/F-34 gun

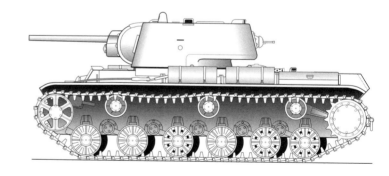

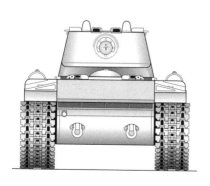

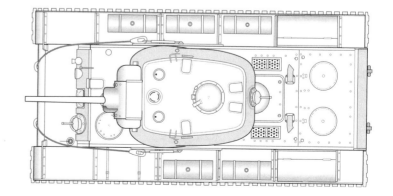

-34/76 Medium Tank (Model 1943) with ChKZ turret

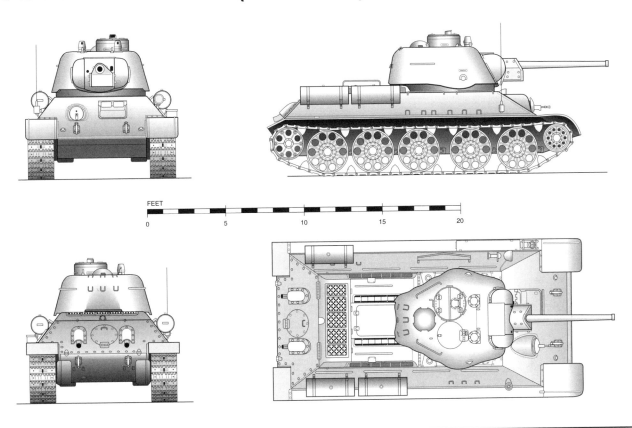

FEET

0   5   10   15   20

KV-1s Heavy Tank

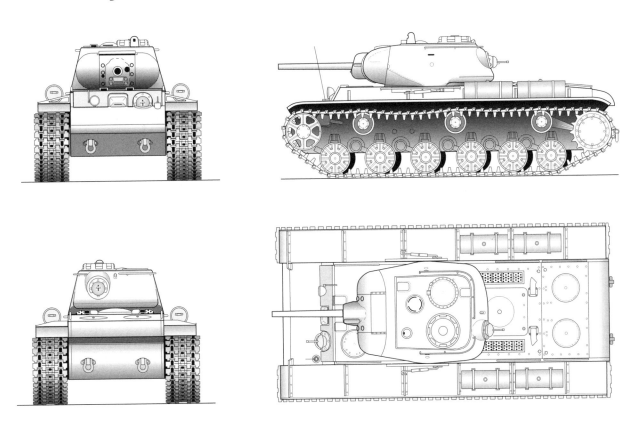

SU-122 Assault Gun (Model 1943) early

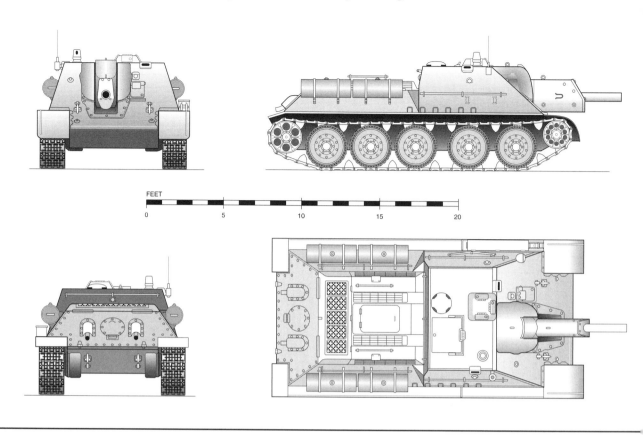

FEET

0   5   10   15   20

KV-8 Heavy Flamethower Tank with 45mm gun

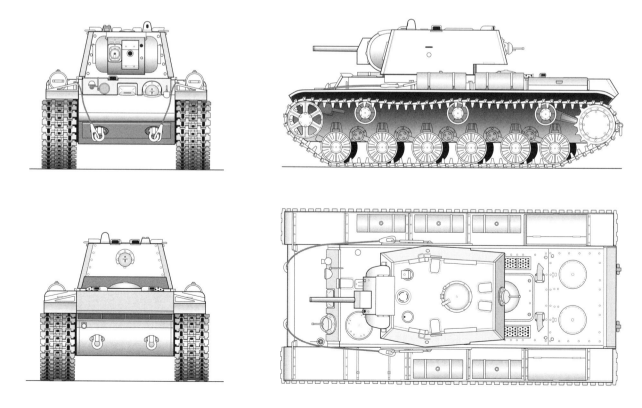

U-76i Assault Gun
n Pz.III chassis

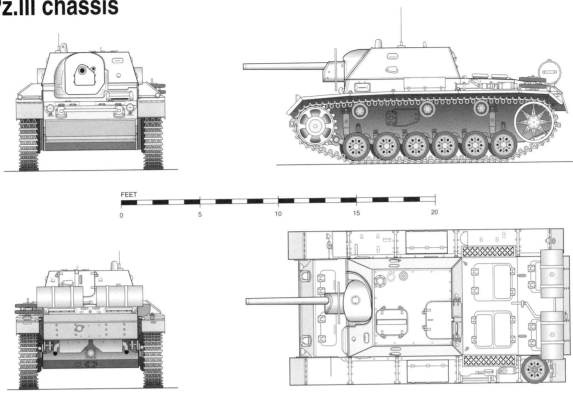

FEET

0   5   10   15   20

3TR-40 Reconnaissance Scout Car
nd Troop Carrier

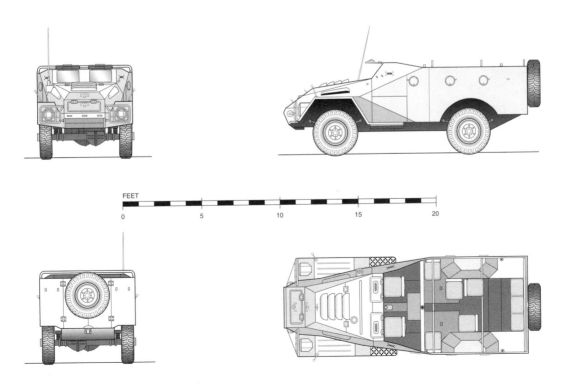

FEET

0   5   10   15   20

T-70M Light Tank

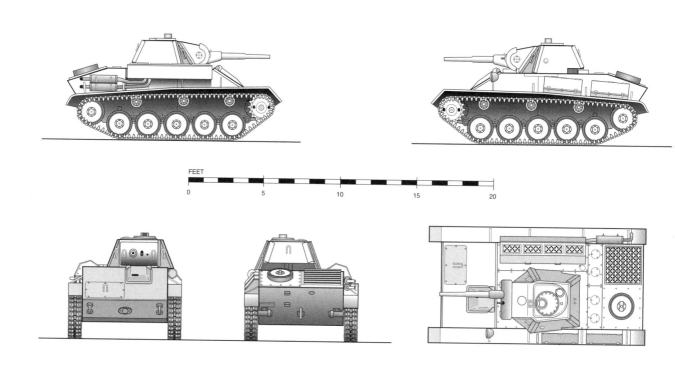

FEET
0   5   10   15   20

SU-85 Tank Destroyer

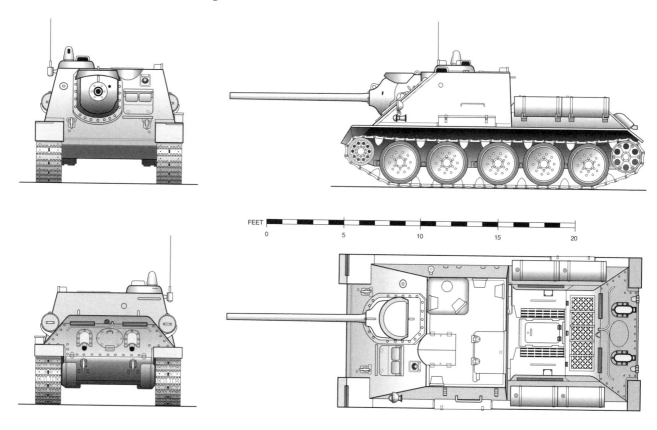

FEET
0   5   10   15   20

U-152 Heavy Assault Gun

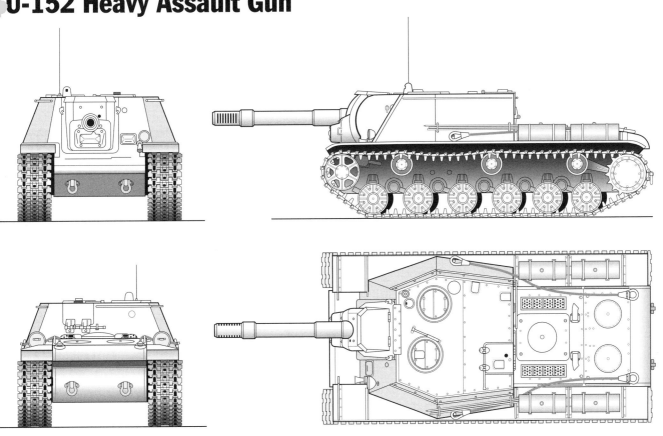

SU-122 Heavy Tank Destroyer

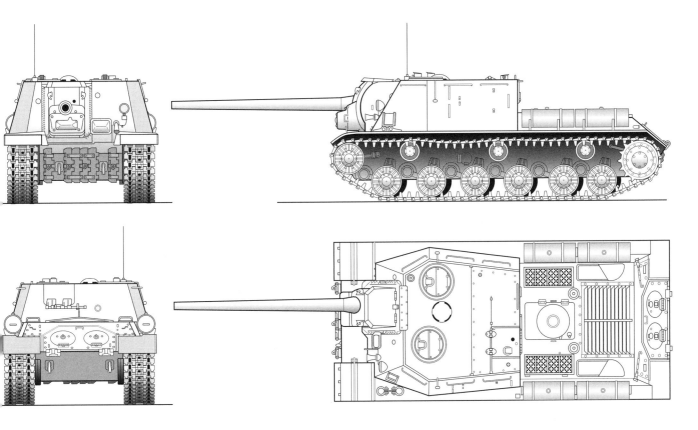

ISU-152 Heavy Assault Tank

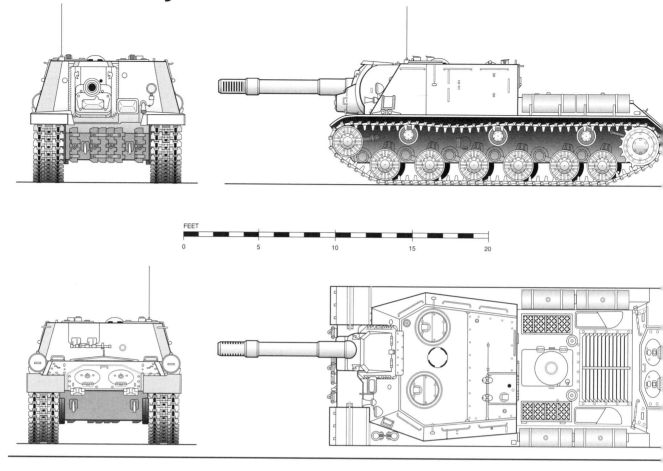

FEET
0   5   10   15   20

SU-76M Self-Propelled Gun (early)

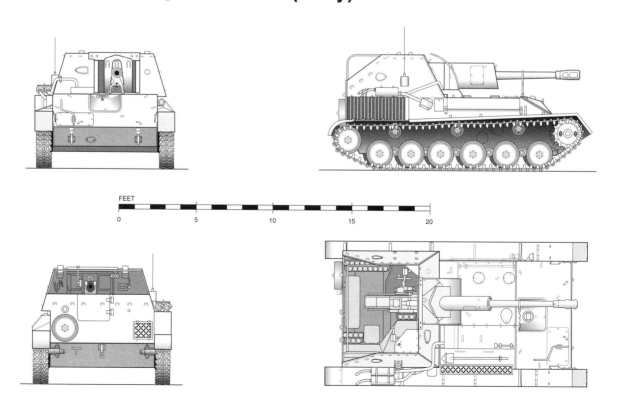

FEET
0   5   10   15   20

KV-85 Heavy Tank

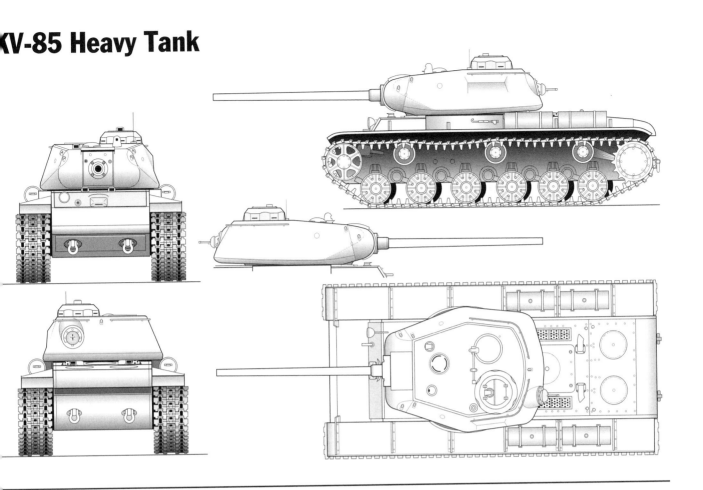

T-34/76 Medium Tank (Model 1943/44)

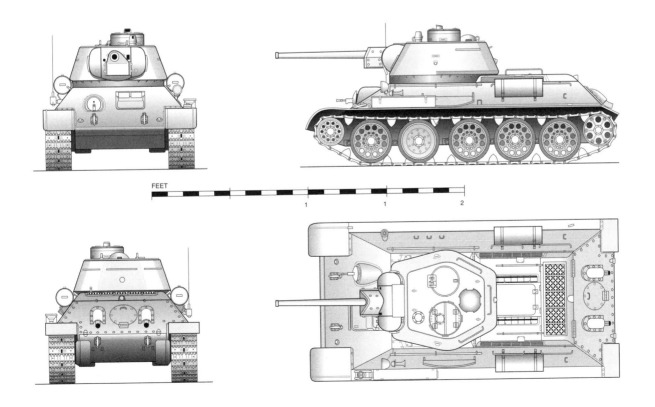

FEET

SU-100 Heavy Tank Destroyer

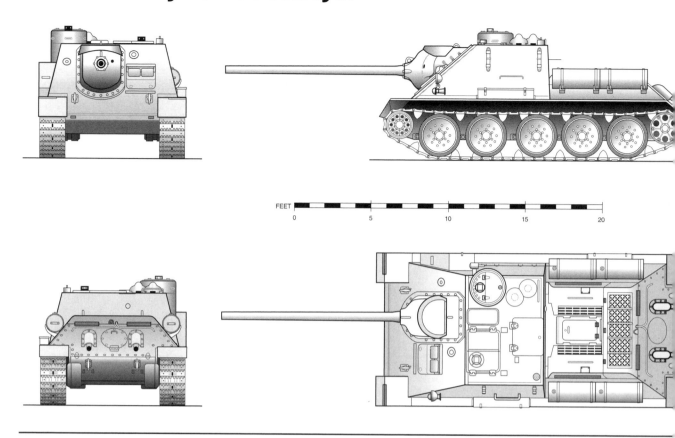

FEET
0   5   10   15   20

SU-76M Self-Propelled Gun (Late Model)

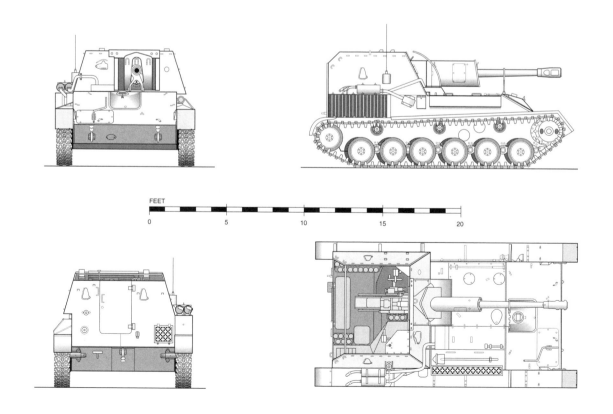

FEET
0   5   10   15   20

-34/85 Medium Tank

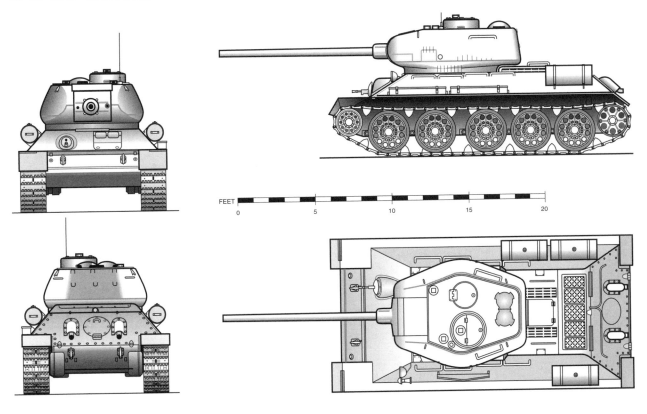

FEET
0   5   10   15   20

T-44 Medium Tank

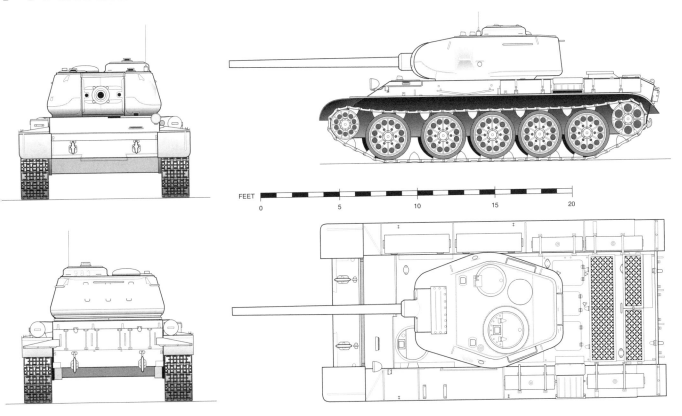

FEET
0   5   10   15   20

IS-2m Heavy Tank

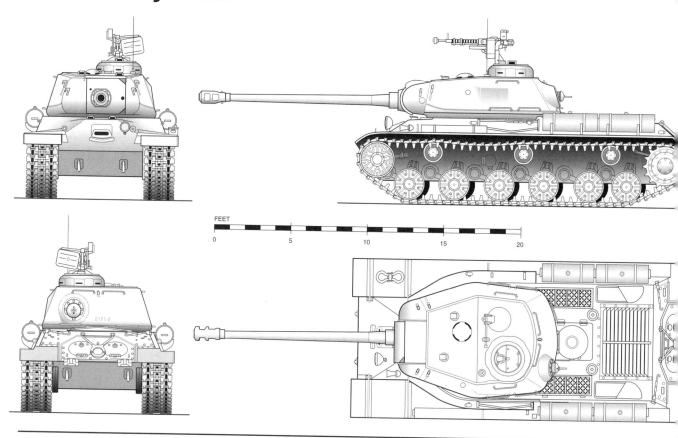

IS-3 Heavy Tank (Model 1945)

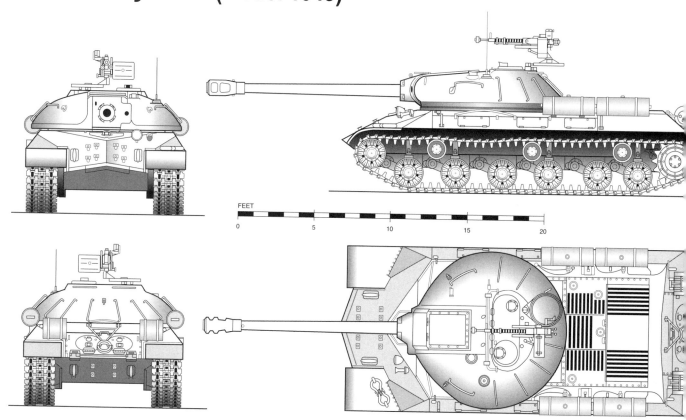

SU-101 Tank Destroyer "Uralmash-1"

Developed late in the war, this type would have
replaced the SU-100 in 1945.

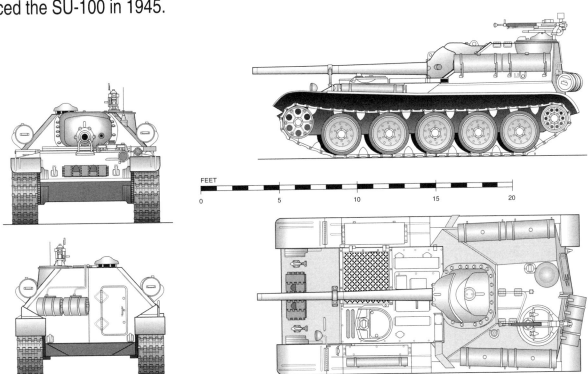

FEET

0   5   10   15   20

Marmon-Herrington Mk. I
Armored Car

The South African-built Marmon-Herrington armored cars proved very important as reconnaissance vehicles in the Western Desert in 1941. The basic chassis for these vehicles were made in Canada by Ford and shipped to South Africa for final assembly and armament at the South African division of Ford Canada. The early hulls were riveted but were later welded. In the British 2nd Armoured Division, at least 50 of them fitted out the 1st Kings Dragoon Guards Armoured Car Regiment in 1941 and served them well.

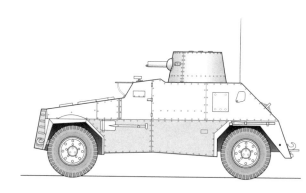

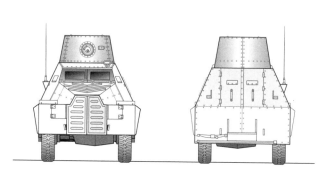

FEET

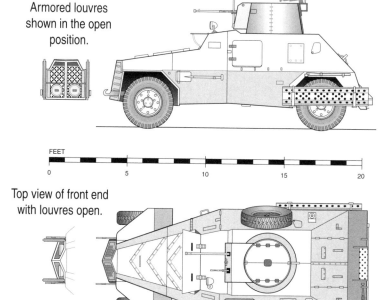

Marmon-Herrington Mk. II
Armored Car (Later Welded Chassis)

The basic turret armament of the Marmon-Herrington Mk. II armored car was the Boys anti-tank rifle, two Bren guns, and a Vickers machine gun. However, a goodly number were upgunned with everything from the Italian 47mm, the German 37mm, the French 25mm, or the Italian Breda 20mm anti-aircraft and anti-tank guns.

Armored louvres shown in the open position.

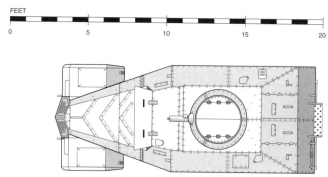

FEET

Top view of front end with louvres open.

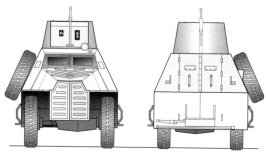

Marmon-Herrington Mk. III
Armored Car

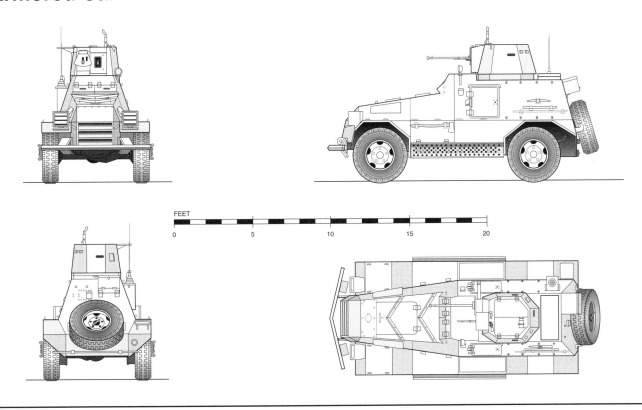

FEET
0   5   10   15   20

Marmon-Herrington Mk. IV
Armored Car

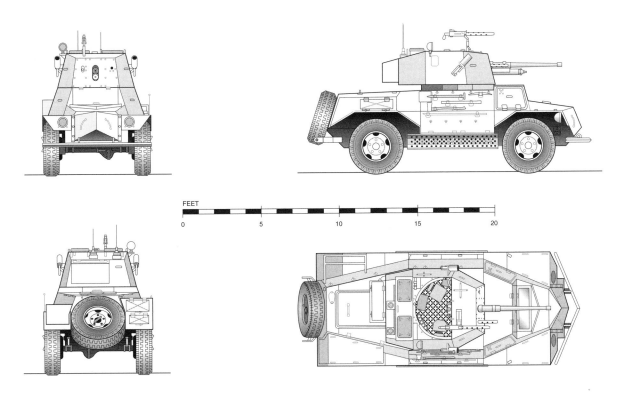

FEET
0   5   10   15   20

BIBLIOGRAPHY

Chamberlain, P., and C. Ellis. *British and American Tanks of World War II*. London: Arms and Armour Press, 1969.

———. *The Churchill Tank*. London: Arms and Armour Press, 1971.

———. *Making Tracks: British Carrier Story*. Windsor, England: Profile Publications, 1973.

———. *The Sherman: An Illustrated History of the M4 Medium Tank*. London: Arms and Armour Press, 1968.

Fletcher, D. *Crusader & Covenanter Cruiser Tanks, 1939–45*. London: Osprey Publishing, 2005.

———. *Mr. Churchill's Tank: The British Infantry Tank Mark IV*. Atglen, PA: Schiffer Publishing, 1999.

———. *Tanks in Camera, 1940–1943*. Stroud, England: Sutton Publishing, 1998.

Forty, G. *A Photo History of Armoured Cars in Two World Wars*. Poole, England: Blandford Press, 1984.

———. *United States Tanks of World War II*. Poole, England: Blandford Press, 1983.

Foss, C. F. *The Encyclopedia of Tanks and Armoured Fighting Vehicles*. London: Amber Books, 2002.

Hayward, M. *Sherman Firefly*. Tiptree, England: Barbarossa Books, 2001.

Henry, H. G. *Dieppe through the Lens*. London: Plaistow Press, 1994.

Hunnicutt, R. P. *Armored Car: A History of American Wheeled Combat Vehicles*. Novato, CA: Presidio Press, 2002.

———. *Half-Track: A History of American Semi-Tracked Vehicles*. Novato, CA: Presidio Press, 2001.

———. *Sherman: A History of the American Medium Tank*. Bellmont, CA: Taurus Enterprises, 1978.

———. *Stuart: A History of the American Light Tank*. Novato, CA: Presidio Press, 1992.

Icks, R. J. *Encyclopedia of Armoured Cars*. Secaucus, NJ: Chartwell Books, 1976.

———. *Encyclopedia of Tanks*. London: Barrie & Jenkins, 1975

———. *Tanks & Armored Vehicles, 1900–1945*. Old Greenwich, We Inc., 1967.

Lemon, C. *Organization and Markings of United States Armored Units, 1918–1941*. Atglen, PA: Schiffer Publishing, 2004.

Perrett, B. *The Valentine Tank in North Africa, 1942–43*. Shepper England: Ian Allan, 1972.

Skulski, P. *Seria "Pod Lupa" 101, T-34/76*. Wroclaw, Poland: Ac Publication, 1997.

The Tank Museum. *Churchill Tank: Vehicle History and Specifica tions*. London: Her Majesty's Stationery Office, 1983.

Touzin, P. *Les Engins Blindés Français, 1920–1945*. Paris, France Collections armes et uniformes, 1976.

———. *Les Véhicules Blindés Français, 1900–1944*. Paris, Franc Editions E.P.A., 1979.

White, B. T. *British Armoured Cars, 1914–1945*. Hampton Court, England: Ian Allan.

———. *British Tank Markings and Names*. London: Arms and Armour Press, 1978.

———. *British Tanks and Fighting Vehicles, 1914–1945*. Shepper ton, England: Ian Allan, 1970.

———. *British Tanks, 1915–1945*. Hampton Court, England: Ian Allan.

Yeide, H. *Weapons of the Tankers: American Armor in World War St. Paul, MN: Zenith Press, 2006.

Zaloga, S. *Armored Thunderbolt: The U.S. Army Sherman in Worl War II*. Mechanicsburg, PA: Stackpole Books, 2008.

Zaloga, S., and J. Grandsen. *Soviet Tank and Combat Vehicles of World War II*. London: Arms and Armour Press, 1984.

Zaloga, S., and J. Laurier. *M3 & M5 Stuart Light Tank, 1940–45*. Oxford, England: Osprey New Vanguard, 1999.

Zaloga, S., and P. Sarson. *IS-2 Heavy Tank, 1944–1973*. Oxford, England: Osprey New Vanguard, 1996.

Basic Tank Components

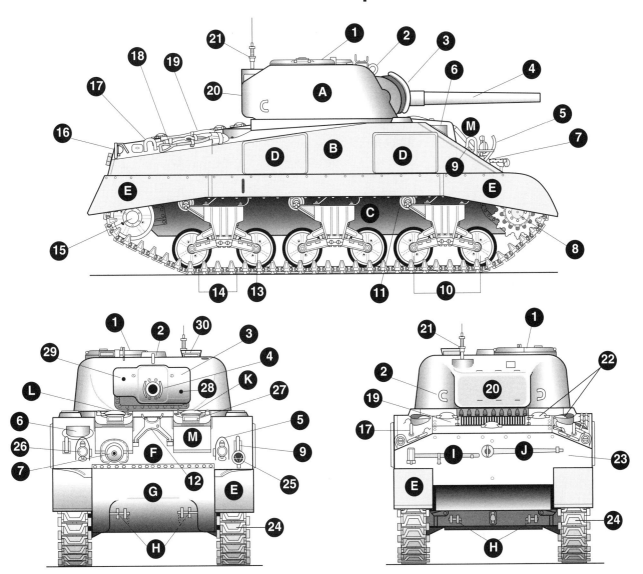

A. Cast Turret
B. Upper Hull
C. Lower Hull
D. Appliqué Armor
E. Dust Skirt
F. Glacis Plate
G. Transmission Housing
H. Towing Brackets
I. Sledge Hammer
J. Idler Adjusting Wrench
K. Driver's Hatch
L. Ass. Driver's Hatch
M. Angled 1" Plate

1. Commander's Hatch
2. Turret Lift Hook
3. Gun Mantlet
4. Main Gun
5. Headlamp Guard
6. Ventilator
7. Bow Machine Gun
8. Drive Sprocket
9. Hull Lift Hook
10. Bogie Suspension Unit
11. Trailing Return Roller
12. Gun Lock
13. Road Wheel
14. Track Links
15. Rear Idler Wheel
16. Tail Lights

17. Chassis Lift Hook
18. Tools
19. Engine Deck
20. Turret Bustle
21. Radio Aerial
22. Fuel Filler Caps
23. Rear Plate
24. Track Shoe
25. Siren
26. Driving Light
27. Driver's Periscope
28. Coaxial Machine Gun
29. Main Gun Sight
30. Loader's Periscope

VARIOUS MODELING SCALES

Scale	1 inch equals	1 scale foot =	1 scale meter =	Comments
1:4	4"	3"	250.0 mm	Flying Models, Live-steam Trains
1:8	8"	$1^{1}/_{2}$"	125.0 mm	Cars, Motorocycles, Trains
1:12	1'	1"	83.3 mm	Cars, Motorcycles, Dollhouses
1:16	1' 4"	$^{3}/_{4}$"	62.5 mm	Cars, Motorcycles, Trains
1:20	1' 8"	$^{19}/_{32}$"	50.0 mm	Cars
1:22.5	1' $10^{1}/_{2}$"	$^{17}/_{32}$"	44.4 mm	G-Scale Trains
1:24	2'	$^{1}/_{2}$"	41.7 mm	Cars, Trucks, Dollhouses
1:25	2' 1"	$^{15}/_{32}$"	40.0 mm	Cars, Trucks
1:32	2' 8"	$^{3}/_{8}$"	31.25 mm	Aircraft, Cars, Tanks, Trains
1:35	2' 11"	$^{11}/_{32}$"	28.57 mm	Armor
1:43	3' 7"	$^{9}/_{32}$"	23.25 mm	Cars, Trucks
1:48	4'	$^{1}/_{4}$"	20.83 mm	Aircraft, Armor, O-Scale Trains
1:64	5' 4"	$^{3}/_{16}$"	15.62 mm	Aircraft, S-Scale Trains
1:72	6'	$^{11}/_{63}$"	13.88 mm	Aircraft, Armor, Boats
1:76	6' 4"	$^{5}/_{32}$"	13.16 mm	Armor
1:87	7' 3"	—	11.49 mm	Armor, HO-Scale Trains
1:96	8'	$^{1}/_{8}$"	10.42 mm	1/8" Scale Ships, Aircraft
1:100	8' 4"	—	10.00 mm	Aircraft
1:125	10' 5"	—	8.00 mm	Aircraft
1:144	12'	—	6.94 mm	Aircraft
1:160	13' 4"	—	6.25 mm	N-Scale Trains
1:192	16'	$^{1}/_{16}$"	5.21 mm	1/16" Scale Ships
1:200	16' 8"	—	5.00 mm	Aircraft, Ships

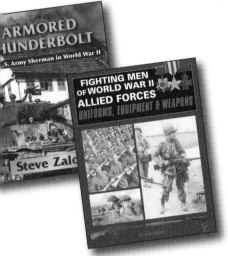
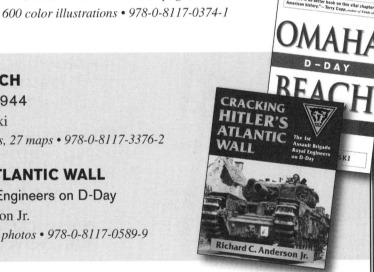